**NEA**
**EARLY CHILDHOOD**
**EDUCATION SERIES**

# Empowering At-Risk Families During the Early Childhood Years

Kevin J. Swick
Stephen B. Graves

**A NATIONAL EDUCATION ASSOCIATION**
**P U B L I C A T I O N**

Printing History
    First Printing:    May 1993

**Note**

The opinions expressed in this publication should not be construed as representing the policy or position of the National Education Association. Materials published by the NEA Professional Library are intended to be discussion documents for educators who are concerned with specialized interests of the profession.

**Library of Congress Cataloging-in-Publication Data**

Swick Kevin J.
        Empowering at-risk families during the early childhood years/ Kevin J. Swick, Stephen B. Graves.
            p. cm. — (NEA early childhood series)
        Includes bibliographical references.
        ISBN 0-8106-0366-7
        1. Home and school—United States. 2. Problem families—Services for—United States. 3. Early childhood education—United States—Education—United States.
I. Graves, Stephen B. II. Title. III. Series: Early childhood education series (Washington, D.C.)
LC225.3.943 1993
362.829--dc20
                                                                        93-7563
                                                                        CIP

# CONTENTS

**The Authors**

Kevin J. Swick is Professor of Early Childhood Education at the University of South Carolina, Columbia, South Carolina.

Stephen B. Graves is Associate Professor of Early Childhood Education at the University of Alabama, Birmingham, Alabama.

# INTRODUCTION

A major social challenge confronting our society is the development of educational and support systems for families. During the past 40 years, several events have combined to create a stress-filled environment for families. New challenges have emerged: AIDS, drug abuse, increasing crime, economic malaise, moral deterioration, and increases in mental health problems (Skolnick 1991). These and other challenges are "new" in the sense that they are now intense and pervasive; they are present in every community in some form. Most people know one or more of these stressors in some concrete form. We may struggle with how to balance our two-career families. Or, we may be the single-parent family struggling to meet the children's economic and social needs. It may be a neighbor whose family has been traumatized by AIDS. It may be our teenage daughter's newborn who is suffering from cocaine withdrawal. In a way never before experienced in our society, every person can sense the intensity of our social problems.

Yet, beneath the surface of these problems are many possibilities for social improvement. For example, many of us have seen firsthand what quality early childhood education is like and what it can accomplish. Our recognition of the positive influence of good parenting is another signal of what is possible in our communities. We have also seen what can be achieved in good schools and caring communities. For example, supportive teacher attitudes and caring adults are positively affecting children's development. The challenges are many, but the potential for achieving a just and caring world is also great.

## NEW STRESSES FOR FAMILIES

The most disturbing element in the social change that has taken place since 1950 is the increasing stress in families. Every generation experiences stress. However, the rapid pace and complex nature of social change in recent times has been dramatic. As a society we have moved from an industrial to an information-based economy, creating jobs and roles unheard of in previous generations. This economic and social revolution has prompted many changes: the emergence of information industries, the transformation of existing industry, the creation of totally new communities (and the dissolution of others), the evolution of a global media system, and the restructuring of the nature and composition of the workplace (Halpern 1987). At the same time, psychological and social change have resulted from new life-span events, such as responding to increased longevity, negotiating psychosocial identity within more complex family arrangements, and relating to the more intense needs of children as they experience higher educational and social expectations (Hamburg 1992).

The magnitude of this change process is experienced most dramatically within the family system. Families have become the "system" by which social change is internalized, adapted, and then activated in society. They provide the vision, energy, and structure by which the change process is negotiated (Skolnick 1991). When the stresses promulgated in the society overwhelm families and create a "high risk" for dysfunction, the result can be a loss of vision, energy, and structure for the society at large. In effect, the foundation of the society is threatened when the family system is placed in a high-risk position.

The increase in stress experienced by families since 1950 has been dramatic. Increments in family dissolution, child abuse, teen-parenthood, alcohol and other drug abuse, and other family pathologies are cause for alarm. These symptoms reflect more than family responses to normal change processes. They indicate basic structural changes that have emerged over the past 40 years. In particular, economic change has been a major stress. The real decline in wages, increased demands for highly educated workers, and the increased cost of raising children (as well as caring for older parents) have combined to create an untenable situation for most families (Gibbs 1990, Hewlett 1991). Economic stress has caused other family dynamics (role changes, structural refinements, and relationship changes) to be more intense.

# OUTMODED SOCIAL SUPPORT

While families have been enmeshed in revolutionary social change, they have not received needed support for effectively coping with it. As Bronfenbrenner (1979) notes, while we have changed the economic and social landscape of the community, we failed to assist families in making the needed adjustments. The reality is that most of the risks we now confront are of our own making. Outmoded economic, legal, social, and family practices and policies are major sources of the stress we face. Skolnick (1991, pp. 200-201) offers some examples of this society-family mismatch.

> Still other difficulties are a result of the mismatch between the new realities of family life and social arrangements based on earlier family patterns. For example, the problem of "latchkey children" could be remedied if we had the will to do so—through after-school programs, or a lengthening of the school day, or flexible work schedules for parents. And at least some of the painful consequences of divorce are products of the legal policies and practices governing the dissolution of marriage. No-fault divorce is a classic case of unintended consequences: what looked like reform of an unfair, degrading way of dealing with marital breakdown turned into an economic disaster for older homemakers and mothers of young children. Yet here, too, the worst features of the system can be remedied—for example, by postponing the sale of the family home until children are grown.

As a society we are indeed the creators of the at-risk conditions in which families find themselves, and ultimately it is "we" who can rectify these conditions.

Children under six and their parents are the citizens who have and are paying the biggest price for the social revolution of the past 50 years. This is true for children and parents across the various social, economic, and cultural dimensions of our society. They are the poorest of the poor, the most isolated from social support, and have the least amount of power to affect needed policy changes (Edelman 1992). Just as disturbing is the fact that a majority of parents and their children believe that their quality of life has declined. Even families who have not suffered economically point to a decline in family time, deteriorating moral values, and decreasing community support as alarming. They also feel "at risk" with regard to their health and well-being. Beyond the immediate problems, families and researchers depict a negative view of the future. In a synthesis of current thinking about the future of families, Skolnick (1991, p. 213) states:

The future these researchers foresaw offered less economic opportunity, greater risks of downward mobility, fewer public efforts to respond to social needs, and a widening gap between haves and have-nots. Under these circumstances, people would experience greater stress and anxiety than at any other time in America's postwar history.

## Families and Schools

Not surprisingly, our society has looked to two historical sources for dealing with the dynamics of social change: the family and the school. Unfortunately, social action has not matched the social rhetoric to support families and schools in an effort to create a more viable community. For example, many social ills are blamed on families, not the system that has failed to support families. Schools face a similar predicament. They are expected to both secure and advance the values of the society. Yet, unless schools are supported in altering their system, positive social change is not likely. As the dynamic forces that occur within the family-school-community mosaic change, the underlying "systems" by which these social units function must also change. A few examples of how this process has been distorted over the past 50 years help to explain how the "at-risk family syndrome" has emerged.

Throughout this century the move toward new economic realities has been under way. The last 30 years have included dramatic shifts in the way families function economically. A

10

majority of families are now "two-wage earner" operated. Plus, parents typically work longer work weeks for less pay, usually attain more schooling and training to achieve and maintain their job status, spend more time out of the home than within family relationships, and acquire more of their psychological and social identity within the workplace (Hewlett 1991). These structural changes have influenced the family system in various ways: in reduced time for marital and parent-child relations, an increased need for out-of-home child care, a need for more flexibility within marital and family roles, and the need for major changes in the way family decisions are made (Swick 1987).

While the social and economic demands on families have increased, social arrangements for supporting families in dealing with these changes have not been forthcoming. Cowan and Cowan (1992, p. 22) describe particular aspects of this double bind:

> In recent decades there has been a steady ripple of revolutionary social change. Birth-control technology has been transformed. Small nuclear families live more isolated lives in crowded cities, often feeling cut off from extended family and friends. Mothers of young children are entering the work force earlier and in ever larger numbers. Choices about how to create life as a family are much greater than they used to be. Men and women are having a difficult time regaining their balance as couples after they have babies, in part because the radical shifts in the circumstances surrounding family life in America demand new arrangements to accommodate the increasing demands on parents of young children. But new social arrangements and roles have simply not kept pace with these changes, leaving couples on their own to manage the demands of work and family.

The consequences of a "hands-off" family policy have been devastating. Increases in divorce, child abuse, homelessness, and other dysfunctional family behaviors reflect this double-bind predicament. Today's young families are finding it difficult to negotiate daily life with an outmoded social support system.

Schools are also experiencing this "double-bind" situation. Kaplan (1992) notes that every feature of schooling remains inadequate to the new expectations of our society, yet little incentive or direction has emerged to foster a more modern educational system. In the past, schools had a specific and limited mission that was to educate children in basic skills and to sort them into appropriate tracks that suited their likely status as adults. These tasks were easily achievable in predominantly homogeneous communities where stability was more prevalent than change.

Today's schools, however, face a new set of expectations. They are expected to prepare all children for living in a highly complex and ever-changing society. In doing so they are expected to be "in partnership" with families and communities in meeting multiple social and educational needs (Swick 1991). Yet, a factorylike industrial school model still prevails in most settings. Schools still function within time, space, curriculum, and program designs that are more suited to the past than to the present or future. For example, while most of the society now functions on a longer work day, schools remain on a 1950s time frame. Space is still allocated along the lines of the isolated self-contained classroom with grouping and tracking as common practices. Curriculum content, while changing with the times, still lags behind the ever increasingly complex world in which children live. And program designs are just beginning to explore the comprehensive family services approach so urgently needed. While new teacher-training efforts are focusing on family and community needs, a lack of resources to enact these strategies has stymied many schools (Swick 1991).

Ultimately, a new paradigm that is based on a family-school-community learning and support system is needed. The severity of the risks confronting all families is indicative of this need. The education and development of children is too important to be "pieced out" to selected groups; it must be integral to everyone's mission. To achieve this need, early childhood educators must pursue activities that promote a partnership with parents of young children.

## FOCUS OF THIS BOOK

The focus of this book is on strengthening the early childhood educator's position in creating supportive relationships with families, particularly with those who are in at-risk situations. First, the book outlines the basic elements essential to understanding the needs of at-risk families. Included in this understanding is the importance of taking an ecological-empathetic approach to supporting families. In such an approach, the professional recognizes that risks are a part of our complex social system. Various contexts of at-risk families are explored with the emphasis on the key risk areas that face children and families during the early childhood years.

A complementary focus is on positive ways early childhood professionals can support at-risk families. An empowerment approach to family strengthening that includes the concepts of empathy and being an empathetic helper are strongly recommended. The basis for such empathy is in understanding families (within the realities they experience) and in knowing the many dimensions of ourselves as empowering helpers.

The nature of the "barriers" confronting at-risk families, and particular perspectives on how these barriers can be resolved, are also examined. In particular, the realities of these barriers as they negatively influence the lives of children and families is presented within the framework of a social systems perspective. Attention is given to both traditional and emergent barriers. Early childhood professionals are encouraged to study these barriers in light of their approaches to working with families. New perspectives on addressing barriers to family wellness are also discussed.

While at-risk families typically experience common challenges, they do so in unique ways. These unique family responses are explored in a manner that reminds us that "at risk" is experienced differently by each family. The case studies in the book explore the very personal nature of the situations at-risk parents and children experience. They also provide insights from researchers and practioners on ways we can support the families through empathetic strategies. These insights are process-oriented approaches that early childhood educators can adapt and refine according to the situations they face.

Finally, a collection of "empowerment strategies" for use in strengthening at-risk children and parents is described. These strategies are placed within an ecological-empathetic framework and are offered as a means of developing positive family-school relationships. Some of the themes emphasized are: "Strategies That Empower," "Teacher Roles for Empowering Families," and "Toward a Framework for Empowering."

The major goal of this book is to promote new ways of thinking about and relating to families, with the focus on strengthening families and family-school relationships. The need for more empowering relationships within families and for their involvement with schools and communities is evident. The "risks" they face are risks that have long-term implications for every facet of our society. Early childhood educators have an historical commitment to the well-being of families. We hope the ideas presented in this book will further strengthen this commitment and offer today's professionals some new strategies to use in their efforts to strengthen families.

# Chapter 1

# AT-RISK FAMILIES: THE CONTEXT

During the past 50 years, two perspectives have emerged that provide early childhood educators with new insights and strategies for better relating to the needs of children and parents during the early childhood years. They are the ecological/empathetic perspective and the perspective of "risk."

## THE ECOLOGICAL-EMPATHETIC PERSPECTIVE

While the *ecological-empathetic perspective* has a continuing historical foundation, it was with Bronfenbrenner's publication of *The Ecology of Human Development* (1979) that this perspective became popularized. The basic tenets of the concept are that individuals or family units are influenced by the events and experiences that occur in their lives (their ecology) and that these events and experiences can be understood and influenced to promote healthy modes of development and learning (empathetic strategies). This perspective, while not denying the importance of individual behavior or of genetic influences, fosters a more comprehensive perspective regarding family living (Albee, Bond, and Monsey 1992).

The concept uses the following framework for approaching the study of families: all human systems are comprised of elements that enable them to function; human systems are connected to other systems in a transactional manner; the elements within a human system influence each other; and human systems strive to maintain their "integrity" through a needs-resources balancing process (Swick 1987). Within this perspective, the development of individuals and families is seen as a dynamic process of person-environment relationships. In this sense, the child's behavior (as well as the family's) is seen as a part of a set of interrelated "systems" (physical, social, economic, spiritual, psychological, ecological) that have a powerful influence on each other. For example, a child's passivity toward learning may be influenced by several person-environment factors, such as malnutrition, abuse, poor health, family needs, or combinations of these and other factors (Garbarino 1982, Ford and Lerner 1992).

The "empathetic" element of the ecology of human development provides the understanding dimension of how children and families function (Swick 1987). It is based upon the premise that human behavior has a purpose and that this purpose is influenced by what happens within the person/family system as it relates to other social systems (Schwartzman 1985). In effect, human behavior can be understood and thus supported in achieving healthy and productive modes of living. By "understanding" (being empathetic to) what is happening in families and assessing possible influences on the family's status, strategies can be designed to promote its well-being. Through empathetic perspectives, early childhood professionals hope to become sensitive to observable and subtle strengths as well as to needs within the family system.

## THE CONCEPT OF RISK

The *concept of risk* evolved within the study of the ecology of family development and functioning, especially with regard to the family's development during the early childhood years. The term *risk* is appropriate as it implies that possible harm may come to the individual or family with regard to the nature of particular stressors. It recognizes that all individuals and groups are, in some sense, at risk. It also provides a basis for viewing family strengths and needs within a systems framework (Swick 1987).

Through the study of children and families, it has been noted that certain conditions or attributes put individuals and groups at risk (Garbarino 1982, Schwartzman 1985). Researchers have consistently noted that when certain conditions were present (such as extreme poverty or low-resource social contexts), the individual and/or family integrity was threatened (at risk)

16

(Dimidjian 1989). In this sense, risks function like "stressors" in that they often require an inordinate amount of attention in order to maintain a level of adequate functioning. Left unattended, they erode the family and/or the person's system for carrying out development and learning (Honig 1986).

Family and individual integrity are comprised of four key elements: self-esteem, a sense of mastery, meaningful social supports, and a belief system that is characterized by a sense of faith and optimism (Garbarino 1982, Gordon 1975, Schaefer 1991, Swick 1987). These elements function as an integrated, dynamic foundation upon which families develop their identity and power to grow and find meaning (Swick 1987). When these elements are threatened by stressors that erode self-esteem, reduce mastery, destroy meaningful social supports, and reduce one's faith in life, the potential for family dysfunction is great.

The power of unattended stressors is greatest during the early childhood years (Bronfenbrenner 1979). While all people confront risks, their power to destroy the fabric of meaningful relationships is most evident in the family's formative years. In particular, the concept of at risk, as it is used in early childhood education, indicates the child and family are experiencing conditions that threaten their immediate and long-range well-being (Garbarino 1982, Pence 1987). These risk situations have their sources in both environmental and constitutional contexts and are usually the outcome of the interplay of forces within these contexts.

The conceptual framework (Bronfenbrenner 1979; Dunst, Trivette, and Deal 1988; Powell 1989) of an ecology of human learning and development support new perspectives in examining factors that create risk situations. As Bronfenbrenner (1979) has noted, most family studies of the past focused mainly on the dyad and often were carried out in laboratory settings or other artificial contexts. Further, the majority of these studies were simplistic cause-effect efforts that never accounted for many significant events that were indeed influencing the family.

In contrast to past constructs that focused on a single factor or were delimited, the ecological perspective focuses on multiple influences and the dynamics of these influences as they take place in various person-environment contexts (Pence 1987, Ford and Lerner 1992). In this sense, the meaning of at risk takes on a changing nature, related to many possible combinations of events as they continually interact to influence individuals and groups. It provides a broader perspective for attempting to understand how human beings learn and develop. It also provides a foundation upon which proactive, empathetic strategies can be explored in relation to enabling children and families to seek control over their lives (Dunst, Trivette, and Deal 1988). For example, in exploring family influences on children's school success, it is now recognized that parental self-esteem, belief systems, the family's sense of social support, and an actualization of optimism (faith) in life are very powerful. Families have many strengths that can be actualized when the ecology is supportive.

Beyond the power of the family, evidence is emerging that school supports can empower at-risk children and their parents (Comer and Haynes 1991). For example, in a recent analysis of the low-participation patterns of at-risk parents, Swick (1991a) noted that the presence of an intimate informal helper often buffered the child from the full force of negative stress. The informal helper often provided the child with positive alternatives to the negative factors in his or her setting. While the helper could not change all of the debilitating conditions that existed, he or she could support the child, actively engage the child in positive experiences, and attempt to promote these experiences within the family.

## DIFFERENTIATING LEVELS OF RISK

Developmental and ecological thought recognizes that all persons and groups confront risks at some point in the journey. Evolving from this perspective is a framework for seeing riskness in light of possible levels of severity as well as from the sources of influence (Comer and Haynes 1991, Garbarino 1982). While each individual and family experience riskness in unique ways, there are degrees of intensity that help professionals to better understand and support children and families. *Low risk* implies that the individual or group is not seriously threatened. While one or two risk conditions are present, they are not intensive and do not appear to dominate the individual or group's energy. *Moderate risk* implies that two or more serious risk conditions are present, pervasive, and do represent a distinct threat or potential danger to the individual or group. *High risk* indicates the individual or group is indeed experiencing events that place integrity and functioning at risk (Swick 1987, 1991b). Children and families in the highest risk category usually are confronting multiple stressors that combine to influence their lives in a pervasive and debilitating manner. For example, homeless families are often experiencing many events beyond and yet interrelated with homelessness: poverty, illiteracy, desertion, unemployment, poor health, and so on (Towers 1989a). Further, the individual or group is experiencing events that place integrity and functioning at risk (Towers 1989a). Children and families in the highest risk category usually are confronting multiple stressors that combine to influence their lives in debilitating ways. Risk conditions have many sources within the person-environment process: individual and family resilience factors (such as self-esteem); intergenerational factors, such as family histories, mental health patterns, and constitutional attributes (i.e., health and wellness); and socio-ecological factors, such as the economic stability of society, the social structure of society, and cultural influences (Garbarino 1982).

Combined, the concepts of an ecological-empathetic approach to learning and development and the paradigm of at risk provide a structure for effectively relating to the needs of children and families. In particular, these concepts support a sensitive approach to relating the needs of all families to the contexts in which development and learning take place.

# UNDERSTANDING THE CONTEXTS OF AT-RISK FAMILIES

There are many factors that have the potential to create *a context of risk* for today's families: poverty, illiteracy, malnutrition, poor health, inadequate support systems, drug abuse, unemployment, and multiple combinations of these factors (Caldwell 1989, Garbarino 1982, Pence 1988, Swick 1987). It is important to recognize that each person and each family experience these risks in unique ways. We must also recognize that while risk factors can and often do degrade families, the inherent worth and goodness of children and parents remains constant (Blazer 1989).

The goal is to understand what is happening to families in high-stress situations and to then create empathetic-ecological strategies that support their growth through resolving or modifying these forces. One way to initiate this process is to acquire an understanding of both the "context indicators" and the "behavioral indicators" of children and families who are at risk.

*Context indicators* are those factors that permeate the environment of families who are experiencing (or are likely to experience) stressors of a risk nature, especially as they are related to their social and emotional relationships (Kerr and Bowen 1988). For example, an alcoholic family is in a context that has many stressful indicators: severely impaired social and emotional relationships, passive/aggressive individual and group tendencies, poor work and family functioning, and often a "sense of isolation" from their surroundings. Figure 1.1 lists some of the context indicators in at-risk families.

These context indicators usually function in an interactive manner; two or more of them exist as influences on the development and learning of children and families (Dimidjian 1989). It is important to note, however, that the presence of these indicators alone does not equate with at-risk family conditions. Rather, depending on the nature of the indicators (substance, severity, longevity) and the sources of stress underlying them, a condition may exist or emerge to negatively influence the family (Thompson and Hupp 1992). Some context indicators are more powerful than others, especially at particular points in the life span. For example, while malnutrition is always a negative stressor, it is most damaging during the early years of life (Dimidjian 1989, Woolston 1991). This same observation holds true with regard to the formation of social and emotional health in children and families (Swick 1987). In effect, research clearly points to the highly negative influence of risk conditions during the family's formative period of development (Pence 1988). Like any growing organism, the family is most vulnerable during this embryonic period.

**Figure 1.1**
**At-Risk Family Context Indicators**

| | |
|---|---|
| Physical Pathologies | Malnutrition |
| Drug Impairments | Chronic Health Problems |
| Extreme Poverty | Chronic Isolation |
| Severe Family Dysfunction | High-Risk Community |
| Illiteracy | Chronic Unemployment |

There is another significant, but often overlooked, process that occurs when young families are placed in at-risk contexts. This is the process of the social learning system being short-circuited (or destroyed) before it has the time and nurturance to create within itself a sense of wellness and health.

21

When young families are constantly responding to high-stress situations they have little energy for creating a proactive and nurturing family. In such contexts, families who are at risk develop behavior patterns that may be destructive of their integrity and are often dysfunctional (if not antisocial) within the larger environments of school, work, and neighborhood (Schwartzman 1985). Research has noted several behavioral indicators of at-risk family situations.

*Behavioral indicators* are patterns of functioning in the family's life that symbolize their riskness. Figure 1.2 lists some of the more prevalent indicators found in at-risk families. As in the case of context indicators, the severity and persistence of behavioral indicators is the key to their being symbolic of at-riskness (Garbarino 1982). For example, every person has periodic self-doubts; it is the presence of continuing and pervasive self-image problems that is cause for concern. Where a parent is so insecure that he or she fears rejection at every turn in the life course, his or her self-esteem is clearly at risk. Likewise, an isolated family conflict is probably an indicator of healthy change taking place (e.g., a family member experiencing a new event in life).

Yet persistent and pervasive family abuse indicates dysfunction and indeed symbolizes riskness (Swick 1987). In effect, the nature, longevity, and severity of behavioral indicators provide the clues to the extent of risk that individuals or groups may be experiencing. Consistent antisocial behavior, severe cognitive dysfunction, excessive socioemotional disorders, and distinct developmental delays usually are symbolic of risk behavior, particularly when they appear in multiples over a continuing period of time (Magid and McKelvey 1988, Thompson and Hupp 1992).

Context and behavioral indicators are often interrelated, creating an ecology that may promote a continuing spiral of riskness (Dimidjian 1989, Kerr and Bowen 1988). Examples of

22

**Figure 1.2**
**At-Risk Family Behavior Indicators**

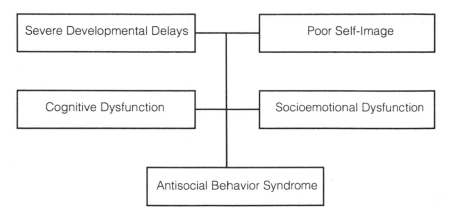

the relationship between context and behavioral indicators can provide insight into the complexities inherent in the process of riskness. Magid and McKelvey's (1988) description of Antisocial Personality Syndrome is one of the better examples of this construct. In this syndrome, the individual's antisocial behavior (aggression, theft, abuse) is "symbolic" of a context that includes various debilitating stressors, such as detachment, neglect, abuse, poverty, and illiteracy. What emerges from an initially small dysfunctional relationship system is a spiraling ecology of risk in which antisocial behavior becomes the norm and continually erodes healthy attributes that might exist in the environment, which in turn further influences the development of additional antisocial behaviors.

A similar process exists in the ecology of drug-abused babies (Shores 1991). Not only is the prenatal cocaine-exposed infant subject to the biological impairments that often accompany this syndrome, but he or she is also likely to experience the many other context and behavioral maladies that seem to permeate the drug environment. In a sense, mothers who expose the fetus to drugs are themselves often victims of high-risk ecologies. As Stone (1990, p. 3) writes:

Girls who suffer physical and sexual abuse or neglect may enter sexual relationships very early in life, in a desperate search for affection and security. As poor, single mothers, they sink deeper into poverty, until drugs like alcohol and cocaine seem to offer the only escape from wretched lives.

While the intricacies of the dehumanizing process of riskness are unique in each situation, the pattern is similar across these individual cases. The addicted mother is often embedded in a context in which illiteracy, poverty, abuse, and a myriad of other stressors prevail (Shores 1991). The baby is not only biologically at risk but his or her total ecology is filled with potential life-threatening risks.

## THE RESPONSIVENESS FACTOR IN AT-RISK FAMILIES

The ability to mediate the negative influences of particular events is crucial in both the prevention and resolution of family problems (Swick 1987). This process is called the responsiveness factor. It is an important force in the family's system as related to mediating the interplay between and among context and behavioral stressors.

As Werner (1987, p. 40) notes, it is the interaction of multiple stressors and the individual or group's inability to respond to these negative forces in a functional way that creates a serious risk ecology.

A low standard of living increased the likelihood of exposure of the child to both ecological and psychological risk factors. But it was the joint impact of constitutional vulnerabilities and early family instability that led to serious and repeated delinquencies in both lower-class and middle-class children on Kauai.

The low-responsiveness threshold (usually the result of serious risks, such as family instability) of families allows poverty to unleash its full force on children. A high-responsiveness mode can buffer the negative aspects of riskness. Werner (1987, p. 41) provides an example of how this process can occur.

> We had not anticipated the considerable influence of alternate care givers such as grandparents, siblings, aunts and uncles, parents of boyfriends or girlfriends, on the children and youth in this cohort group. The emotional support of such elders or peer friends was a major protective factor in the midst of poverty, parental psychopathology, and serious disruptions of the family unit.

This same process occurs in the lives of many single parents. Hetherington (1979) noted that single parents who lacked the support of at least one other adult friend confronted more complexities and stress in responding to the challenges of family and personal living.

Pence (1988) observed similar stress-related conditions in families with fewer resources. For example, he noted that families who had few options (due to poverty) with regard to child care were much less likely to take the initiative in seeking child-care alternatives.

The responsiveness factor plays a major role in how parents and children deal with various risks. For example, research suggests that high-support fathers increase the responsiveness focus of mothers toward their infants (Cowan and Cowan 1992, Stern 1977).

Other research shows that parental involvement is influential in "buffering" children from early delinquent behavior (Spivack and Cianci 1987). Strong community life and positive schools also promote resiliency in children (Benard 1992). Education and support services can function as mediating forces in the at-risk family's journey toward empowerment. And an understanding of the key risk areas that often permeate the lives of families can have significant benefits.

# KEY RISK AREAS DURING THE EARLY CHILDHOOD YEARS

Research on families during the early childhood years indicates there are eight key risk areas that threaten the integrity of children and families (Garbarino 1982, Thompson and Hupp 1992). While these risk areas are negative influences throughout the life span, they are particularly damaging when they permeate the lives of parents and young children during the formative years (Bronfenbrenner 1979, Thompson and Hupp 1992). The risk areas are: ineffective parenting, inadequate home-learning environment, illiteracy, poor health care, malnutrition, lack of job skills, and abusive family situations. These factors are embedded in a system where context and behavior indicators interact with each other to create potential or real negative stress on parents and children.

## Poverty

Poverty is one of the prevalent risks in the lives of young children and is also one of the most powerful forms of degradation. It not only reduces the family's ability to respond to its own basic needs, but also increases the potential for exposure to other risks, such as malnutrition and poor health (Garbarino 1982, Thompson and Hupp 1992). In effect, it sets into motion a pattern of living that can (if left unchecked) foster other stressors, such as family abuse, illiteracy, and alcohol and drug abuse. A cycle of dysfunctional relationships may then emerge where parents feel helpless in the face of what appear to be insurmountable problems. In isolation, poverty can be confronted through social and educational strategies. It is the relational nature of poverty with other ecological and developmental risks that appears to degrade family living in intense ways. In today's society, the complexities of poverty are broader than the traditional image of shortages of physical resources; it is also inclusive of spiritual and ecological resources. Dimidjian (1989, p. 31) describes some of these new complexities as they influence families during the early years:

A drive through the borough shows the social signs of a community in disarray. Boarded-up homes, for-sale signs, and buildings in disrepair pocket the area. Young families who are able to relocate, often leave empty a home that has housed three generations. Families who have not been able to make a transition to new employment and a new community—like Sean's—attempt to cope.

The coping process typically involves dealing with *new poverty fallout,* such as a continual loss of income, long-term unemployment, and the related social and emotional stress that accompany this syndrome.

In far too many cases, the poverty syndrome (like other risk syndromes) produces multiple behavior indicators in children and parents: severe developmental delays in children's cognitive, physical, social and emotional development; dysfunctional adult behaviors related to alcoholism, depression, and a myriad of psychosomatic pathologies; and overall family disintegration (Stevens and Price 1992). Risk syndromes appear to have their most degrading influence on the very source of the family's power base, their collective relationship system. It is through the "relationship system" of the family that stressors are mediated, where the many internal and external challenges that threaten family integrity are articulated and resolved (Kerr and Bowen 1988). When this system of coping is seriously damaged, family strength is eroded. Clearly, parental competence to respond to risk factors is paramount.

## Ineffective Parenting

Ineffective parenting is the most serious risk confronting families during the early childhood years. Parenting is the key mediator by which families carry out problem solving, form relationships, and develop affective and instrumental processes integral to their development. Swick (1987) identifies four elements that comprise effective parenting (parent integrity): self-image, locus of control, self-other relationships, and social support. A weak or negative self-image, low internal control, negative and/or abusive self-other relationships, and a low-support ecology are distinguishing attributes of ineffective parenting. Combined, these elements influence parental behavior in ways that increase the potential of risk factors emerging within the family's environment. (See Figure 1.3.) For example, low self-esteem in parents has been observed as highly related to various family dysfunctions, such as abuse and neglect. Not surprisingly, low self-esteem in parents is usually interrelated with ecological factors in their context: low support, illiteracy, and personal-historical experiences with abuse and neglect (Edelman 1987). A cycle of interactional (and possibly intergenerational) experiences (neglect, insecurity, ineffective parenting, and other at-risk indicators) appears to create a *culture of riskness.* Low-resource family environments and abusive family ecologies are prone to generate more abuse and dysfunction (Schorr and Schorr 1988). As Fraiberg (1977) notes, dysfunctional parents focus their energy on "defining themselves," trying to sort out the underlying sources of their insecurity and chaos. Such self-absorption leaves little room for responding to the needs of others in an effective manner. Lacking in proactive social and cognitive skills, ineffective parents tend to respond to stress in defensive and irrational modes. This web of parent incompetence is often embedded within social contexts that reinforce incompetence. Essential to the fostering of more functional parenting are interventions that enable parents to create contexts that support healthy family relationships (Hamburg 1992). The possibilities of shaping such interventions are many.

Figure 1.3 presents one possible scheme for addressing the needs of at-risk parents. Fraiberg (1977), in working with detached mothers found that attachment therapy/counseling was

## Figure 1.3
## Risk Area: Ineffective Parenting

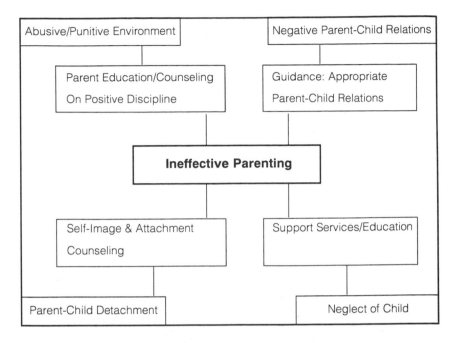

effective in mediating the stress of one's own personal inadequacies in relationship to the nurturance of infants. In this case, mothers needed to resolve their images of themselves (which most often evolved from their own abusive contexts as children) in order to create the needed sense of nurturance in their relationships with their infants. Results of a similar nature have been observed in other parent education and family-support activities. Powell (1989), for example, observed that the informal social experiences of parents involved in parenting programs served to broaden their social context and increase their resources for parenting. Pence (1988) also noted the possible benefits of parent/family education programs for increasing parents' social support resources. Clearly, the most dramatic role that parent education, appropriate parent and family counseling, and family support activities can play is one of *prevention*. White (1988) has documented the specific child competence gains as well as parent and family variables (relationships, life-style, literacy) that appear to emerge within families when well-designed parent-education programs are available and used.

## Inadequate Home-Learning Environments

Inadequate home-learning environments (often interrelated with ineffective parenting) is another major risk factor during the early childhood years (Bronfenbrenner 1979). While there are degrees of inadequacy in any home-learning ecology, families at risk often lack literacy materials, consistent rituals for nurturing healthy relationships, an interest in learning, a social system for sustaining learning, resources to promote wellness, and strategies for fostering a positive social and emotional environment (Garbarino 1982, Stinnett 1981, Swick 1987). It is important to note, however, that many at-risk families effectively mediate this source of stress through the creative use of the environment. In effect, the strength of parental competence can be a positive antidote to the sources that may promote inadequate home-learning contexts (Swick and Graves 1986). For example, work with low-risk families (Swick 1991a) has found that a lack of literacy materials in the home can be mediated through instigating stronger leadership in parents (assisting parents in finding needed literacy resources), and by involving them in continuing parent-education programs. More intensive parent/family involvement projects have noted various parent behaviors that mediate the family's literacy status. This includes accessing community resources (joining and using the library), taking advantage of home-learning resources, developing regular family literacy rituals, using available finances for learning resources for the family, and engaging in continuing dialogue with the child on learning and literacy activities (Epstein and Dauber 1991, Rich 1989).

In high-risk families where multiple sources of inadequate home learning interact (family dysfunction, poverty, isolation, illiteracy) to degrade the system's resiliency, the challenge is more complex. (See Figure 1.4.) Particular context and behavior outcomes of such ecologies have been noted. These include cognitive delays, developmental disabilities, language delays, and social and emotional dysfunction (Sartain 1989). Research is consistent on the most viable mediating force: parental efficacy (Schaefer 1991, Swick 1991b). Parental mastery of basic family learning and key parent-child social and emotional relationship patterns are integral to the forming of effective home-learning arrangements.

Four mediating strategies early childhood educators have found useful in preventing or resolving the stressors inherent in inadequate home learning are: involving parents in learning and using home-learning strategies, providing parent training opportunities, carrying out diagnostic/support services for families on an individualized basis, and promoting positive social and emotional learning patterns within the family (Edelman 1987). Each of these strategies has potential to directly and/or indirectly alter the family's ineffective home-learning patterns.

**Figure 1.4**
**Risk Area: Inadequate Home Learning**

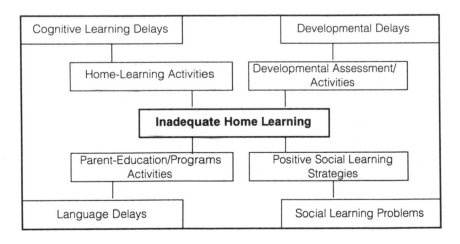

Gordon's (1975) observation that parent training and family-support activities not only improve parent-child relations but also appear to foster improved parental self-esteem is one example of the power of these strategies. Comer and Haynes (1991), Powell (1989), and Rich (1987) have noted several parent behaviors indicative of an emerging positive focus on home learning that have evolved in conjunction with these strategies: increased parental involvement at home and school, more responsiveness to children's interests, expansion and strengthening of the family's social context, increased attention to family learning time, continuous completion of home-learning activities, and parental involvement in educational enrichment activities.

The evidence suggests that when parents and children are encouraged to engage in home-learning activities in meaningful ways, they capitalize on these opportunities. A key to this mediating process is respect for family integrity and the role that parental leadership plays in family learning (Pence 1988). What is also apparent is the need to recognize the multiple stressors that influence ineffective home learning; that is, the realities of each family's unique situation must be addressed as these strategies are deployed (Swick 1991a).

## Illiteracy

A major stress that influences ineffective home learning is illiteracy. (See Figure 1.5.) Often interrelated with other risk indicators, it functions as a central element of continuing and intense stress (Dunst, Trivette, and Deal 1988). The inability to use cognitive processes in effective ways limits a person's problem-solving skills, erodes self-confidence, impedes relationships with others, and ultimately imprisons the individual (and very likely the family) within a closed-circle ecology. Perhaps the most extensive damage illiteracy perpetrates is on the interpersonal fabric of family relationships. Unable to carry out positive communication and support behaviors, many negative indicators may emerge: abuse, poor attitudes toward learning, and cyclical behavior patterns of a passive-aggressive nature (Garbarino 1982). In addition to these degrading influences, are possible adult outcomes that further generate this cycle: persistent unemployment, low self-esteem, lack of parenting skills, and related dysfunctions (Dimidjian 1989).

**Figure 1.5**
**Risk Area: Illiteracy**

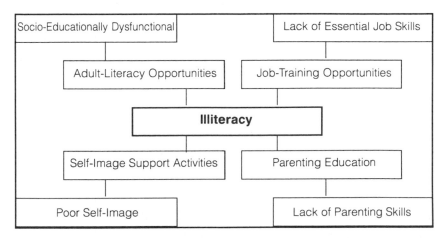

As Figure 1.5 indicates, mediating influences can buffer and/or position parents to achieve reasonable levels of literacy. There are, however, some underlying premises that need recognition for literacy strengthening strategies to have the best possible influence on families.

One premise is that we recognize that all people already have some form of literacy skills that they use to function within their environment (Dunst, Trivette, and Deal 1988). For example, nonreaders have often been observed doing reading behaviors when in the security of their culture. Typically, illiteracy refers to one's inability to function effectively within the macrosystem culture. Professional helpers need to distinguish between types of literacy so that their perceptions of people are focused on the strengths that do indeed exist (Swick 1991b).

Another premise is the realization that invitations to literacy are indeed a sharing of learning opportunities that require a supportive approach. Far too often "helpers" expect invitations to be readily accepted, not recognizing the tremendous investment of trust required in this process of growth. Illiteracy is not the equivalent of distrust. Rather, it is a context and behavioral situation that the individual must choose to alter.

This leads us to another premise, that of valuing the person and the family without regard to particular cultural, constitutional, or environmental realities. Our valuing a person's presence without any preconditions is itself an invitation to grow. It should also lead us toward a better understanding of the strengths, innate goodness, and the potential of children and adults in risk situations, and even develop a deeper appreciation of our own strengths and needs (Swick 1984).

It is also critical that literacy strategies, such as adult education, job training, parenting education, and related activities, reach parents during the family's formative period of development. Work with teen-parents, for example, does indicate that their completion of high school and/or related job training increases their overall functioning as parents (Powers 1985). Even short-term literacy projects where parents and children engage in shared-learning experiences have shown both an immediate increase in parent-literacy activity and extended involvement of parents in experiences of a literacy nature (Swick 1991a).

## Poor Health Care

Poor health care threatens the entire family's well-being, particularly during the early childhood years. (See Figure 1.6.) Poor nutrition, lack of self-care skills, inadequate sanitation, lack of access to health care, and inadequate health-literacy skills create stressors that degrade the family's cognitive, physical, social, emotional, and spiritual development (Powers 1985, Boyer 1991). While health care and health status are clearly interrelated with other risk factors, such as poverty and illiteracy, they are emerging as a threat to young families in all social and cultural contexts. The U.S. Department of Education (1988) reports that indicators, such as alcohol/drug abuse, suicide, and AIDS, are on the rise, appearing across social and economic lines. Further, wellness indicators, such as physical activity, religious participation, involvement in school enrichment experiences, positive life values, and proactive health behaviors, are on the decline among adults and children (U.S. Department of Education 1988).

Health and wellness are the fabric of strong families and healthy societies (Stinnett 1981). When this fabric is damaged in any family member, the entire family is at risk, at least within the context of their intrarelationships (Dunst, Trivette, and Deal 1988). For example, malnutrition and poor health care can create severe stress in the child and in turn negatively influence the family's evolving wellness (Blazer 1989). Lack of knowledge and skills related to maintaining adequate health care (among parents) is correlated with serious problems in young children, such as hearing impairments, chronic infections, nutrition-related maladies, and a plethora of social and behavioral dysfunctions (White 1988, Woolston 1991). Perhaps the most severe damage to the child and the parent is the emergence of a pessimistic outlook on life. In effect, what may initially appear to be a risk may then evolve to embrace the family within a degrading cycle of poor health, family abuse, and antisocial behavior patterns (Thompson and Hupp 1992).

Mediating strategies that promote proactive health and wellness habits need to be pursued extensively with families who have very young children. (See Figure 1.6.) The emphasis must be on preventive strategies young families can acquire and integrate into their family-living pattern. Health education combined with involvement in establishing good health and wellness habits does reduce the potential negative influence of

## Figure 1.6
## Risk Area: Poor Health Care

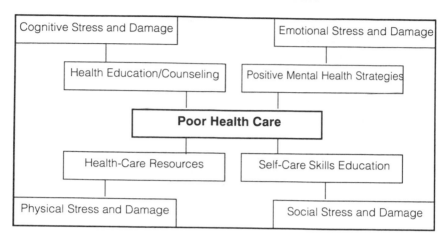

health stressors. Reductions in hearing, vision, and other related health problems occur when children receive appropriate preventive and corrective services. (White 1988, Thompson and Hupp 1992). And immunizing children against debilitating and killer diseases eliminates significant health stressors as well. Of utmost importance, is the promotion of self-management and self-care skills in parents of very young children. Proactive, optimistic approaches to family health-care by parents is the most powerful influence on the family's long-term wellness (Thompson and Hupp 1992). In particular, the mother's prenatal care is critical (Hamburg 1992).

*Malnutrition*

Poor health and poor nutrition are highly related. During the early childhood years, malnutrition is among the risk factors most damaging to the child's development and learning. (See Figure 1.7.) It also wields a powerful social influence because eating and mealtime are intimate processes that engage parents and children in many "relationship building" experiences. In this sense, nutrition and family relationships are interactive forces

36

that influence each other and all aspects of the family's well-being (Thompson and Hupp 1992).

**Figure 1.7**
**Risk Area: Malnutrition**

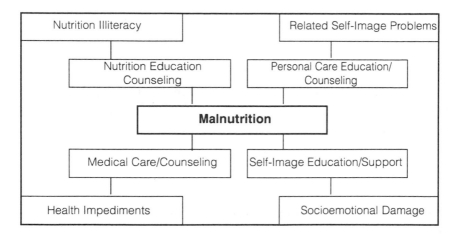

Proper nutrition is highly related to the family's overall life-style. Factors that can mediate the family's nutrition and wellness orientation include nutrition education, personal care training, proper medical care, and self-image counseling and support with trusting helpers (Hamburg 1992). Various combinations of these strategies have been used effectively during the early childhood years, influencing maternal and child health in observable ways. Improved parent attitudes, weight gains among children, and healthier family relations are a few of the indicators present in the research (Garmezy 1992).

## Lack of Job Skills

Poverty and illiteracy create a context for inadequate job skills, which in turn, often contribute to unemployment and/or underemployment. (See Figure 1.8.) While the intricacies of such negative scenarios vary, their negative influence on parental competence and family viability is dramatic (Dimidjian 1989). Unable to find sustained employment or to project a long-range "image" of themselves as contributing members of a family or community, many of these parents become engaged in a cycle of passive (continuing welfare dependence) and/or antisocial (illegal or illicit employment) behavior syndromes that further erode their entire family's sense of integrity (Schorr and Schorr 1988). For example, research has linked illiteracy that results in sustained unemployment with antisocial, passive-aggressive behavior syndromes (Wilson and Herrnstein 1985). Further, the two major risk indicators of intergenerational family dysfunction are illiteracy and a lack of adequate job skills. Macrosystem analyses of social program impact on long-term improvements in family and community living indicate context and behavioral change are best achieved through literacy, job training, and employment strategies (Schorr and Schorr 1988).

**Figure 1.8**
**Risk Area: Lack Of Job Skills**

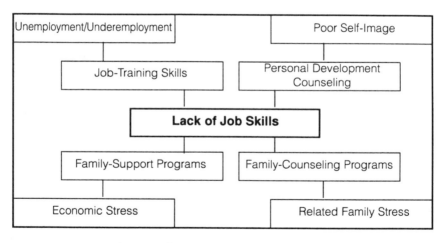

An ecology of empowerment that includes literacy opportunities, job training, individualized family support-strategies (i.e., child care and family health-care) and parent/family counseling can be a powerful antidote to breaking the cycle of inadequate job skills, poverty, and illiteracy. These sources of power not only increase the parents' employability but they also strengthen their position as family leaders. For example, the Kenan Family Literacy program (Darling 1989) found that parents acquired skills that went beyond the desired job placement sought; they learned how to better manage family time, set priorities, and develop more positive interpersonal family-relationship styles. Clearly, these are skills applicable to parenting and family life. In addition, the contexts in which parents acquire job skills often introduce them to other supportive arenas, such as adult friendship-networks, counseling, and "mentoring" possibilities (Powell 1989).

*Abusive Family Situations*

Abusive family situations, whether of a self-inflicted nature (chemical abuse) or of a group-sustained structure (child or spouse abuse), place the entire family in a high-risk context (Garbarino 1982). The realities of family abuse reveal that these contexts often include combinations of self- and other abuse syndromes. For example, drug abuse is clearly linked to other abusive behaviors within the family. (See Figure 1.9.) It is destructive of healthy family dynamics at any point during the life span (especially during the early childhood years), disrupting parent-child attachment experiences and preventing the emergence of healthy family bonding behaviors (Burgess and Streissguth 1992). In place of healthy family relationships, various pathological syndromes take hold and create a dysfunctional family arrangement (Schorr and Schorr 1988). These syndromes include addictions of various forms, antisocial behaviors, severe developmental delays, and a plethora of other pathologies (Magid and McKelvey 1987).

## CHEMICAL ADDICTIONS

In particular, various chemical addictions, as they are played out within the family, can create a mosaic of problems for everyone. Towers (1989b, pp. 7-8) states:

> Alcoholics and drug addicts hurt those around them by destroying family stability, unity, and security. At its worst,

alcoholism/addiction can result in loss of income, loss of self-respect, spousal and child abuse, and divorce. For the children, it can lead to delinquency, substance abuse, and suicide. At the very least, children of alcoholics/addicts will suffer feelings of low self-esteem, shame, fear, and loneliness; and they may grow up lacking in the ability to trust and develop relationships with others. It will certainly affect how well they function in school.

This process is most damaging during the early years. For example, research on "crack babies" indicates that the mother's addiction is often imposed on the infant, bringing with it several retarding influences: possible brain damage, disruption in the attachment process, neurological damage, and a myriad of other problems (Shores 1991). Accompanying these problems are various family stressors, such as the dysfunction of the parent, unstable (and often chaotic) relationships among family, and the multiple antisocial behaviors, that are a part of the drug culture (Griffith 1992).

Mediating strategies that have proven successful in addressing the drug-addiction risk include: rehabilitative treatment, supportive medical counseling (often integrated into rehabilitation efforts), parent and family support resources, and related family-empowerment services (Towers 1989b). Recent interventions have focused on the ecological complexities of family-addiction indicators as opposed to the isolated treatment of the "addicted" person. This focus has aided the entire family in seeing the social system as contributing to co-dependency and thus in need of therapeutic efforts. In this sense, the addiction is or can become a family affair. To resolve only the chemical dependence syndrome may not have much long-term impact on personal/family relationship patterns (Griffith 1992).

What needs to be unearthed is the web of social and emotional dynamics at the foundation of the person's chemical dependence. The addiction serves only as a fragile and artificial

40

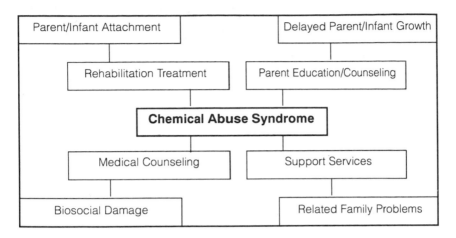

**Figure 1.9**
**Risk Area: Chemical Abuse Syndrome**

| Parent/Infant Attachment | Delayed Parent/Infant Growth |
| Rehabilitation Treatment | Parent Education/Counseling |
| **Chemical Abuse Syndrome** | |
| Medical Counseling | Support Services |
| Biosocial Damage | Related Family Problems |

buffer from what may appear to be a quite painful reality. A major focus of intervention (and prevention) must be attending to the perceptions of everyone involved in the addictive process as well as to the intricate network of pathological interactions that typically accompany this syndrome. Mediating strategies must attend to all of the factors that are present within the ecology of addiction: the parent's sense of despair as well as his or her drug dependence; the physical, psychological, and social and emotional damage inflicted on the child; the pathological behaviors that emerge within the family; and on using long-term strategies that support the healing process (Tower 1988b, Shores 1991). Prevention education in schools is the most promising "best practice" for the long-range resolution of this risk.

## CHILD/FAMILY ABUSE

An addictive co-dependent, nonchemical risk that is just as damaging is child and family abuse. (See Figure 1.10.) Parents who themselves have experienced abuse or who are a part of a cycle of intergenerational violence often replay this syndrome (Bradshaw 1988). Attributes, such as rigid behavior patterns, physical aggression, psychological abuse, severe neglect, and

41

sexual abuse, are symbolic of deeply engrained insecurities, low self-esteem, and poor mental health (Kerr and Bowen 1988). For example, it has been observed that mothers who themselves experienced abuse (or are currently experiencing it) have serious problems in forming healthy relationships with their children (DeV. Peters, McMahon, and Quinsey 1992). Their lack of an "image" of how to nurture as well as an absence of a sense of being nurtured can block the essential relationship patterns necessary for forming attachments (Fraiberg 1987; Wolfe, Wekerle, and McGee 1992). Research suggests that continuing, pervasive, and interrelated stressors, such as drug abuse, poverty, illiteracy, and severe unemployment, promote parental abuse syndromes (Thompson and Hupp 1992).

Abusive parents (and abusing families) generate an ecology in which family pathologies, severe developmental delays and/or impairments in children, child and adult antisocial behaviors, and extensive abuse syndromes are likely to emerge (Thompson and Hupp 1992). Individual and family dysfunctions related to abuse are numerous, but the most denigrating include physical injury cycles, persistent social isolation, and pervasive spiritual erosion. Abusive parent/family contexts appear to create a closed-system in which recursive abuse patterns are modeled, practiced, internalized, and then extended to internal and external family relationships (Craig 1992). Various studies have described the dynamics of abuse as it permeates not only the family members' interactions but also their relationships at school, at work, and within other social contexts (Garbarino 1982, Dimidjian 1989). The pervasiveness of abusive family syndromes is such that it is often observed within intergenerational patterns. Abusive and antisocial behaviors become accepted as a way of life and even acquire a status among some adults.

Mediation has had some success through the use of family and individual interventions. Kerr and Bowen (1988) have substantiated the value of engaging families in "behavioral self-assessment" in an effort to help family members establish

42

**Figure 1.10**
**Risk Area: Child/Family Abuse**

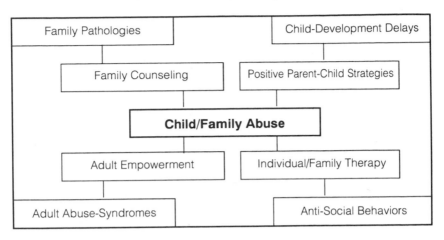

healthier ways of relating to each other. This therapy focuses on helping families see their recursive, closed triangles of abusive relationships and the sources of this enmeshment. The goal is for family members to perceive their dysfunctional relationships and their sources, and to then shift energy toward resolving the stressors at the foundation of the abusive syndrome. Fraiberg (1987), in carrying out a similar process at an individual level, found that detached mothers were able to reconstruct "images" of themselves as worthy persons. This same philosophy is guiding the work of family-empowerment efforts in early childhood education. Dunst, Trivette, and Deal (1988) emphasize the importance of the person or family at risk, seeing the riskness as a need that must receive attention. Thus, mediation strategies must engage families in supportive efforts to acquire self-insight into the realities of their situation. This ecological-empathetic perspective is present in family counseling, parent training, and adult-empowerment support strategies. For example, recent parent-education programs are using a parent-developed "contract" process as a means of engaging parents in articulating their perception of the family situation. The complexities of stressors and the family dynamics involved in abuse are so vast that no single mediation strategy is satisfactory. This is particularly true where family stressors are multiple and chronic in nature (Garbarino 1982, Thompson and Hupp 1992).

## AN ECOLOGY OF HIGH-RISK FAMILIES

The most alarming attribute of high-risk families is the "ecology of despair" that so often prevails (Blazer 1989). Taken in isolation, particular risk features, such as poverty or illiteracy, can be effectively mediated through combinations of educational, social, and economic support strategies. Yet when these risks are embedded in a human relationship system that is characterized by despair, powerlessness, isolation, and extreme insecurity, the potential for creating a "culture of riskness" is very high (Dimidjian 1989). Given a low-resource environment, few options for strengthening context, and a pessimistic view of life, high-risk families often cling to recursive behavior patterns that appear to insulate them from disaster. However, these behaviors usually erode their sense of efficacy and further embed them in a cycle of dysfunctionality. For example, an unemployed father who seeks comfort in excessive alcohol use may then isolate himself from meaningful family relationships. In an effort to gain some sense of power, he may then increase his alcoholism and begin abusive behaviors with the family. Left unchecked, this pattern can soon become a cycle in which the family's social system becomes engulfed in alcoholism and the multiple pathologies that accompany it (Towers 1989b). There are several attributes commonly observed in this cycle of despair (Garbarino 1982, Kerr and Bowen 1988, Pence 1988, Stevens and Price 1992). These include:

- a belief system that is predominantly fatalistic,
- a context that exudes a very low sense of control,
- behaviors that are reflective of low self-esteem,
- a closed and unresponsive relationship system,

- behavioral syndromes that symbolize rigid, passive-aggressive cycles of family interaction,
- a cognitive structure that promotes impulsive, nonreflective thinking,
- an isolated social system,
- a spiritual fabric that lacks a sense of meaning,
- recursive and negative relationship patterns,
- poor problem-solving skills, and
- abusive and antisocial behavior.

These attributes are interactive by their very nature, thus reinforcing a continuing and usually pervasive cycle of riskness. For example, highly impulsive thinking appears to promote chaotic relationships that lack meaning and encourage further atrophy within the family system. An emergent sense of fatalism fosters an unhealthy reliance on external sources of control that often erodes the family's sense of purpose and negatively influences its system for dealing with stress. Lacking a clear structure for dealing with stress, high-risk families often develop social relationships that are very rigid and based on unrealistic expectations. This fragile relationship system can create attitudes and behaviors that are indicative of a low and negative self-image (Kerr and Bowen 1988, Sartain 1989).

The structure and relationships of high-risk families are characterized by three primary sources of stress that are closely related to the attributes of riskness: serious misconceptions about how individuals and families grow and develop, highly distorted ideas about the roles various family members should perform, and the continuing presence of a sense of fatalism (Anastasiow 1988, Swick 1987, Towers 1989b). When these sources of stress prevail, they foster a system that can destroy the family's integrity. Tragically, these sources of stress can ultimately become stressors unto themselves, creating the basis for intergenerational high-risk behavior syndromes (Magid and McKelvey 1987).

The belief that families simply happen without thought and that children develop without serious guidance is a cross-cultural, subtle, and yet devastating source of stress for many families. While the need for parent and family nurturing would appear to be an accepted practice, it is not ingrained in our cultural thinking. As Bradshaw (1988) notes, the repetition of dysfunctionality in families over several generations is an outcome of the mentality that recursive relationship patterns are adequate ways of functioning. Within this mind-set, abuse, neglect, and other pathologies can become accepted patterns (Dimidjian 1989, Thompson and Hupp 1992). The pattern of family dysfunction as described by Bradshaw (1988) includes rigidity in how people function, denial of basic esteem needs, lack of self-differentiation, closed family-relationship patterns, and punitive-cold response styles. These dysfunctional behaviors generate a culture of suspicion and distrust that dehumanizes the individual and the family. Dysfunctional behaviors are learned within the intimate ecology of interpersonal living, often reinforced by cultural forces present within the setting. Swick (1987) reviews several research strands that note that families in which healthy relationship patterns are prevented from emerging by rigid, cold, and punitive dynamics usually create excessive stress that degrades and erodes the family's integrity. In this pathological context, fear and hostility take the place of nurturance, with both attributes igniting further extensions of these distorted relationship patterns (Magid and McKelvey 1987). For example, observations of abused children confirm that their escalating passive-aggressive behavior patterns extend across contexts, such as the school (Dimidjian 1989). These dysfunctional syndromes are usually characterized by shame, guilt, denial of feelings, blame, and punitive responses. In such a context, the self is easily disabled, thus blocking the process of differentiation required for healthy growth and development. Healthy relationship patterns (inclusive of love, affection, guidance, and positive role modeling) are critical to the family's development of integrity. This requires a family value-system that promotes mutuality, trust, exploration, sharing, individuality, and teaming (Stinnett 1981, Kerr and Bowen 1988). Lacking

46

in knowledge on how to function in harmonious and yet divergent ways, high-risk families tend to rely on rigidly defined roles. Instead of a "we" environment emerging through positive helping relationships, an artificial and highly insecure "I-focused" ecology takes shape. This self-centered and very narrowly defined role system impedes the development of family bonding (Fraiberg 1987). For example, in cases where family abuse is extreme, it has been found that various role assignments are inappropriately identified for particular family members. In a sense, the developmental pendulum is torn asunder and roles totally inappropriate for children are assigned to them without sensitive thought. A child may be assigned adult sexual or alcoholic role directions that simply attenuate the adult's life-style and create the potential for child pathologies (Towers 1989b). These debilitating and abusive role assignments preclude the growth process (particularly the natural process of self-differentiation) that must occur if secure and loving relationships are to flourish (Swick 1987).

The nature of human development is "growth-oriented," and individuals must have access to environments and people that support them in this endeavor. In families where role-flexibility is discouraged or impeded, riskness and eventually dysfunction is a likely outcome. For example, one person in the family may subtly be defined as the "buffer," carrying out a protective role for the family from the various stressors that arise say from alcoholism or another addiction. In other cases a family member may become "the person" who absorbs conflicting relationships stressors. Often these role assignments become accepted and expected patterns, embracing the family itself in a rigid and unhealthy scenario (Kerr and Bowen 1988). The sources of such role rigidity are interrelated with the family's daily ritual. While all families experience stress, dysfunctional families not only experience excessive stress, but seem to invite it through a counterproductive life-style. For example, Swick (1991a) observed that very high-risk family ecologies were prone toward irrational and negative response patterns, thus extending a simple problem into a set of complex stressors. Sartain (1989) observed this lack of rational decision making in multiproblem children, especially in their performance in school settings.

The continuing presence of destructive behavior patterns in high-risk families is indicative of an ideology of pessimism and negativism (Baumeister, Kupstas, and Klindworth 1992; Sigel 1985). Despair, distrust, and a sense of powerlessness dominate most high-risk family ecologies. These attributes emerge in relationship systems permeated with nonsupport, isolation, extreme stress, and a history of dysfunction (Bradshaw 1988). Pessimism and negativism erode the family's spiritual fabric and promote a context that is fertile for abuse and neglect. As Magid and McKelvey (1987, p. 178) note, the potential for abuse and role distortion is high:

> They have a lot of violence, neglect, and abuse with little likelihood of much bonding. Inconsistency is the overriding characteristic.

They further explicate some of the complexities of family role distortions:

> The net effect is change in the child's normal role in the family from that of consumer of resources to one of provider. This new role isn't familiar to the child, who is bound to fail at it. Parents in this situation often react with frustration and aggression.

A clear need exists for a more ecological-empathetic approach in establishing and promoting a paradigm that empowers families early on in their life journey. Such a perspective can broaden and sustain more comprehensive and sensitive relationships within families and among the family and societal systems that strongly influence the family's identity. Teachers and schools can be a significant part of this family empowerment process.

# Chapter 2

# EMPOWERING AT-RISK FAMILIES

This chapter explores how an ecological-empathetic perspective toward families can help empower both parents and children. The intricacies of "empowerment" as a concept and practice are also explored with the emphasis on mental perspectives, relationship elements, and enabling strategies. A central part of the approach suggested throughout this book is that "at risk" represents a condition that threatens the entire society and one that evolves from the mix of social, cultural, and family transactions. In this perspective, all families confront risks at different points in the developmental scheme; it is the nature of these risks and the resources and strategies families have access to for responding, preventing, and resolving them that is significant in our efforts to empower parents and children (Ford and Lerner 1992, Thompson and Hupp 1992).

## THE EMPOWERMENT PARADIGM

The concept of empowerment is embedded in the work of researchers and scholars who have focused on various aspects of strengthening the ecology of human development and learning.

The work of Abraham Maslow (1968) helped to solidify our understanding of the basic needs that comprise the individual's physical and psychological sources of meaning. In this concept of individual development, the growing person achieves power through the dynamics of a needs-resources process. The person's ability to develop his or her talents and interests is interrelated with his or her potential to grow. Using a hierarchical structure, Maslow portrayed the individual as growing toward self-actualization when person-environment relationships were supportive of this growth process. Major deficiencies in one's support context (malnutrition, detachment, abuse, poverty) threaten the growth process and weaken one's integrity. Clearly, the key risk areas briefly explored in the previous chapter function as major deterrents to this growth process.

Extending and broadening Maslow's perspective is the work of Erik Erikson (1959, 1982). According to Erikson's theory, the developing person progresses through the life span in a cyclical manner, attempting to resolve major psychosocial needs or "crises" that are critical to one's growth. For example, the initial need is to establish a sense of trust in one's self-environment relationship. If this need is not resolved positively, it influences the person's growth in negative ways. Erikson sees this as a highly interactive process, one that is never totally resolved but that is a continuing and critical part of the individual's journey. The critical element in this developmental focus is that the person's resolution of the major social and emotional needs (trust-mistrust, as an example) is in a direction that empowers them, enables them to establish and enrich a faithful perspective of themselves and others.

Bronfenbrenner's ecological theory emphasizes that power emerges from the nature and structure of human relationships (1979). For example, the infant's need to develop trust is actualized within the primary relationship system of the family and yet strongly influenced by other social systems, such as the neighborhood, church, informal social networks, and related sociocultural systems.

Critical to the person's integrity is not only the context of his or her experiences, but his or her perceptual orientation toward these events and processes. In many cases the individual's perceived reality is more important than what may literally be happening to the person. An empowering person is oriented toward events in a proactive and empathetic manner. The intricacies of how people develop their perceptual focus has been the topic of various psychological theorists and researchers (Hampden-Turner 1981). The influences are many: constitutional factors, parental modeling, family-relationship systems, schooling, peer influences, and cultural belief systems (Hampden-Turner 1981). One of the major building blocks of the empowerment process is grounded in perceptual psychology: individuals must generate perceptual maps in which they see themselves as able and nurturing participants in the life process. Because individual needs, interests, social and emotional development, and perceptual orientation evolve within the family ecology, the premises of family studies (particularly family-systems research) are closely related to the empowerment paradigm. These premises include the following: (1) behavior takes place in a systems context; (2) individual development is intimately interrelated with the family's development; (3) family development is systematic; and (4) events that influence any family member have some direct or indirect influence on the entire family system. Within the family relationship system, trust, attachment, self-esteem, social attitudes and behaviors, and many other processes and skills should emerge in a nurturing and inviting manner (Brubaker 1993, Cataldo 1987, Minuchin 1984).

It is within the family ecology that children and parents develop their sense of power. Empowered parents (and an empowering family) have three enabling characteristics: (1) ability to access and control needed resources, (2) ability to make decisions and solve problems, and (3) ability to interact effectively with others in the social exchange process (Dunst, Trivette, and Deal 1988). This concept of empowerment is process-oriented; it is dynamic and interactive. In this sense, every person and every family have power to some degree, otherwise they would be unable to function even in a minimal sense (Kerr and Bowen 1988).

The empowerment paradigm is enlarged and enriched when viewed within a social systems perspective. Dunst, Trivette, and Deal (1988, p. 5) explicate the value of this perspective:

A social systems perspective views a family as a social unit

51

embedded within other formal and informal social units and networks. It also views these different social networks as interdependent where events and changes in one unit resonate, and in turn, directly and indirectly influence the behavior of individuals in other social units. A social systems perspective also considers events within and between social units as supportive and health-promoting to the extent that they have positive influences on family functioning.

This broader context places the family-empowerment process within a comprehensive framework. The context and behavioral risk factors discussed previously are now more visible as impediments to fully enabling the family to achieve wellness. Mediation of family risks, such as through parent education, quality early childhood education, and family-support practices, can be positioned within this paradigm to function as sources of power for parents, children, and families.

## EMPATHY AS FOUNDATION

The empowerment paradigm alters the traditional approach to helping families. In the past, a reductionist form of thinking predominated among family helpers. This mode of thinking focused on simple identification of a family weakness and on a corresponding strategy to resolve it. The helper was the one doing the assessment and shaping the treatment process, without consideration for the perceptions and ideas of the family. Even today this rather limited approach prevails in the working habits of many helping professionals. The real limitation in this approach is that it is almost entirely dependent upon the helper's perceptions and often ignores the family's cultural and individual insights. While short-term progress may occur within this method, long-term goals of family autonomy and strength are neglected (Swick 1987, 1991b).

The construct of empathy includes several elements of perceptual and interpersonal psychology. It implies that one has the ability to understand another person's situation (inclusive of that person's self-assessment) in an ecologically sensitive and comprehensive manner. Such understanding suggests that the professional is able to relate to the other person's situation in a proactive manner, promoting the total well-being of the family members involved. In this sense, understanding connotes the skill of moving beyond traditional stereotypes that act to isolate professional helpers and families. Observations now become mutually formulated insights that evolve from the family's ideas as well as the professional's.

## BECOMING AN EMPATHETIC HELPER

In the empowerment paradigm, helping is defined as the "act of promoting and supporting family functioning in a way that enhances the acquisition of competencies that permit a greater degree of intrafamily control over subsequent activities" (Carkhuff and Anthony as cited in Dunst, Trivette, and Deal 1988, p. 7). Unfortunately, many professional helpers who purport to believe in this concept fail to practice it in an empathetic manner. In effect, it is not simply a process of meeting family needs but the manner in which such needs are met. Becoming an empathetic helper is the essential element in the family-empowerment process.

The dynamics of becoming an empathetic helper are based on how helpers think about and perceive families. This orientation includes three values: that people and families are competent (or have the capacity to become competent), that a lack of individual or family competence is due not only to personal deficits but is reflective of social system inadequacies, and that individuals and families are the ultimate source of control and power in their lives (Dunst, Trivette, and Deal 1988; Swick 1991b, 1992). In other words, the early childhood family-helper thinks and behaves in ways that are proactive, enabling, and empowering.

Perhaps the most substantive aspect of thinking and behaving as an empathetic helper is the notion of high regard.

This is because high regard implies that early childhood educators value having a mutually rewarding relationship with families. Further, it forms the basis for a partnership approach to empowerment that is inclusive of regard for oneself, a sense of mutuality, and a human system for nurturing in self and others the value of positive living (Swick 1991b).

The foundation for being an empathetic helper is in the self-perception of the person. One must have high regard for self in order to understand why others desire to be treated with regard. Swick (1991b, p. 130) highlights this point:

> This sense of self-importance cannot be based on an artificial self-image, where the person is only going through the motions of imaging oneself as important. It must be based on observable attributes, such as taking care of one's health; developing and pursuing one's interests and talents; nurturing one's mental health; planning for self-renewal time; and fostering in one's self an ongoing image of a growing, learning, and healthy person.

Evolving from one's regard for self is the ability to see others as worthy and important. Blazer (1989) takes note of the critical role that mutuality plays in the development of each person's sense of faith in others and in one's self. From our earliest life experiences, we depend upon relationships with others that foster this sense of mutual respect and worth. When it is fully developed, this mutuality of regard promotes situations where early childhood educators and families reach beyond the typical range of sharing and collaborating to approach excellence in ways rarely experienced (Spacapan and Oskamp 1992).

Clearly, the process of becoming an empathetic helper involves partnership skills, communication behaviors, and problem-solving strategies that support the empowerment process.

Partnership skills provide the means by which empathetic relationships are established. In effect, the helper must perceive the empowering process as a mutual undertaking between helper and parents. Such an approach requires that the helper become a trusted confidante of family interests. Meaningful partnerships evolve through open and meaningful communication. Dunst, Trivette, and Deal (1988, p. 52) highlight this issue:

> Effective communication is the name of the game. The principle way to establish partnerships with families is to communicate in a way that treats individual members and the family unit with respect and trust.

Open and honest dialogue is essential to healthy relationships. Far too often at-risk families experience distorted communication contexts where honesty is missing.

The empathetic-ecological construct focuses on process and solutions. It is problem-solving oriented. Empathetic family helpers attempt to understand family strengths and needs, and act in concert with the family in seeking resources and strategies that will empower them (Stark 1992).

## UNDERSTANDING FAMILIES

The term *understanding* is the essence of an empowerment system. It is symbolic of the professional's ethical and humane position that all families are important, worthwhile, and potentially very creative. In this sense, to understand is to engage in supportive and meaningful dialogue and action with families. This moves us beyond the traditional boundary of knowing families through stereotypes that limit and often distort our relationships with them. It is an interactive focus on empowerment that is inclusive of: (1) knowledge about family dynamics and needs, (2) sensitivity to the vast potential present in family learning, (3) active listening with regard to each family's uniqueness, (4) nurturing and trusting relationships with families, and (5) collaborative actions that further strengthen their varying contexts. Early childhood professionals of many different roles and ideologies have historically been dedicated to this goal if not supported by their sponsors in achieving it (Powell 1988).

Many factors, however, can combine to preclude the most beneficial use of this process as a means of empowering families: (1) over-reliance on diagnostic tools that often misconstrue and/or misrepresent the family's true status, (2) a lack of cultural insight with regard to the family's learning style, (3) equating family "risk indicators" with family weakness, (4) overuse of a deficit perspective, and (5) other limited family-assessment strategies (Ascher 1988, Powell 1989, Weiss and Jacobs 1988). While it is essential to pursue the full study of families, an empowerment model calls for perspectives that aim to arrive at the most optimistic and enabling picture of families. This perspective views the notion of understanding as more than passive analysis. It is projected as the active involvement of helpers and families in solution-oriented projects that capitalize on family strengths.

## Perspectives for Promoting Family Empowerment

The understanding process begins with positive attitudes and expectations toward families. It is further developed when professionals sensitively explore the following perspectives.

- Who are the families we serve? What do we know about these families that can empower us to be caring helpers?
- What do we know about ourselves as early childhood helping professionals? How do we think about the families we serve?
- What are the programs, services, and activities we offer families? Are they "enabling and empowering" in that they respond to family-perceived needs?
- How do our program activities reflect family respect and family autonomy? Do we use parent input in the shaping of program activities?

56

- How is the uniqueness of each family's integrity accounted for in our programs? Are there opportunities for helpers and families to learn about each other's needs and strengths?
- What is the predominant view of our staff regarding families and our relationship with families? Is it one of positive, nurturing partnerships, or is it a cynical view?

The answers to these issues emerge in our work with children, parents, and families each day. Swick (1991b) elaborates on three elements of this "understanding families" dimension of empowerment.

1. *Early childhood educators and families need to be intimately involved (as partners) in the planning and nurturing of healthy environments.* Understanding is best achieved through working with another person or group on a common mission. Beginning with the earliest years of the child's life, parents and educators should be interacting, supporting, planning, assessing, and collaborating with each other to create healthy places and systems in which all members of the family-school team can learn (Dimidjian 1989).

2. *Through the creation of dynamic school-family partnerships, a family-centered "curriculum for caring" must emerge and permeate our understanding of the families we serve* (Bronfenbrenner 1979). Such a curriculum needs to address the issues involved in what attributes promote human competence and the many means by which this process can be pursued. Professional renewal, parent education, family-support activities, and many other strategies deserve attention. Through such means many caring elements can be emphasized: (1) the absolute need for individuals who have positive self-esteem, (2) the urgency for having family and citizens who are prosocial and compassionate, (3)

57

the emergence of culturally sensitive citizens, and (4) the social need for more caring and involved adults (Edelman 1992).

3. *The work of families is too critical to be left in the family domain. A community effort at understanding and supporting families is an absolute necessity.* In effect, a human team of family, school, and community learners need to forge a covenant that aims to secure parent and child wellness as a global priority (Hamburg 1992).

In transcending past perceptions and behaviors in our work with at-risk families, early childhood educators need to attend to several skills and strategies: (1) awareness of the powerful risk factors parents and children often confront, (2) insight into how these risks influence the lives of young families, (3) understanding of specific risks present in the lives of children and families we serve, (4) sensitivity to the way parents carry out their uniquely intimate family life, (5) activities that are particularly empowering for families in risk contexts, (6) alliances with members of risk neighborhoods and communities that encourage family strengthening, and (7) communication patterns that lead to truly collaborative relationships with children and families (Swick 1991b).

## Family Empowerment Issues

Following are some of the issues that need our full study and attention.

- What particular risk factors appear as especially dangerous in our family-school-community ecology?
- What are some of the underlying social and economic forces of these risks?
- How are schools, families, and community groups collaborating to take the leadership on these issues in the community?
- What efforts are we making to take note of the

strengths of families in risk situations?

- How are we articulating these family strengths in our work with parents and children?

Research with families in different contexts indicates communication is the key to an understanding relationship. This communication needs to be based on the interpersonal needs of closeness and mutuality. Parents under heavy stress need the closeness that exists in responsive, supportive, and sensitive communication. They also need a feeling of mutuality and togetherness that is only present in relationships that are based on respect (Blazer 1989).

At-risk families need more in-depth resources and skills for organizing and using resources. They need self-esteem tools that enable them to see themselves and their children as able and valuable. Early childhood educator-parent partnerships have found success when their focus emerges from family-perceived needs and are founded upon mutual respect.

## PARENT/FAMILY PERCEPTIONS AND EMPOWERMENT

The most challenging aspect of the lives of at-risk parents and their children is their perceptual orientation toward themselves and others. The experience of many families is one in which their needs and risk attributes are treated as personal or family deficits. Not only do they often experience feelings of degradation but they are often confronted with a community-wide stigma of being a problem family. Additional forces in shaping feelings of powerlessness often evolve in the parents' personal and family histories and/or through past experiences with professional helpers (Lightfoot 1978, Schaefer 1985).

In particular, parental perceptions of their life context and their ability to guide themselves and their children in proactive directions are critical. Parental perceptions form the basis upon which families build their control orientation. A set of beliefs and values evolve from the orientation of parents and children as they are actualized within the family's development (Kerr and Bowen 1988). One's beliefs, perceptions, and human relationship processes are interactive forces that dynamically influence each other.

Parents develop a control orientation (which in turn is grounded in their perceptual orientation) within a person/environment context. Over the life span, many factors influence this context: childhood experiences, education, family of origin, interpersonal dynamics, and cultural and subcultural parameters (LaRossa 1986). Yet, one's status as a parent brings these factors together in an integrative manner through two very important dimensions: one's personal system of functioning and one's ecology of functioning. Personal dimensions that exert a continuing influence include: education; self-concept; marital/friendship relations; work and economic factors; and related constitutional elements, such as health and personality tendencies. Ecological factors include items such as choices the parent has relative to education, income, and other conditions. Available resources one can use to strengthen parenthood also can influence the potential for improving the quality of one's human condition (Brooks 1987, Swick 1987).

Naturally, what happens to parents in their relationships within the family-community system has a major influence on how they perceive themselves. When parents have had continuing experiences that result from poor health, illiteracy, drug-dependency, and other stressors, they often develop perceptions and behaviors reflective of powerless feelings (Burland 1984, Hamner and Turner 1992). Parents relate and react to the people and events in their lives with a belief system that provides a framework for decision making. When this belief system is based on negative self-perceptions, the parent's position for functioning as an effective family leader is greatly weakened (Cowan and Cowan 1992).

Low and/or negative self-esteem will usually indicate a lack of self-differentiation. People low in differentiation tend to lack autonomy and the self-direction skills needed for leadership

60

roles like parenting. Kerr and Bowen (1988, p. 101) provide a description of the person who is at the lowest level of self-differentiation:

> People at this level are so immersed in a feeling world that they are mostly unaware of an alternative. Major life decisions are based on what feels right . . . . The self is so poorly developed that use of the pronoun "I" is confined to narcissistic pronouncements such as, "I want; I hurt; I want my rights." They are incapable of more differentiated statements such as, "I believe; I am; and I will do." This does not imply that people in this range are necessarily selfish. The lack of self is usually manifested in being complete emotional appendages of the relationship system to which they are attached.

Langer (1989) notes that when people see the possibility of choices in their environment, their participation in it increases. In effect, the context early childhood professionals and other citizens promote for supporting parents and families should focus on fostering parent/family power. Contextual factors (particularly interpersonal relationships) play a significant role in parents' development of perceptions.

> If parents sense little opportunity to improve their position in the community and even less chance to impact specific contexts such as the neighborhood or the child-care setting, their perception of the family's future is limited (Swick 1987, p. 19).

At-risk families often actualize behavior patterns and interpersonal relationships that indicate a sense of powerlessness. What is also often present in these families is an expressed or symbolic need to find ways to empower themselves. They appear to be enmeshed in contexts and behaviors that are counterproductive, cyclical, and highly emotive in content and style. For example, a parent's abusive behavior often results from frustration over being unable to develop a personal sense of efficacy

61

(Kerr and Bowen 1988). A pattern of self-need for recognition and efficacy, frustration in meeting this need, rage feelings resulting from the frustration, and abusiveness toward others often become a normative style of living (Magid and McKelvey 1987).

When these patterns of dysfunctional responses become routine, unhealthy triangular alliances are promoted and integrated into the family's daily living (Kerr and Bowen 1988). For example, alcoholic families form co-dependent triangles where mother-father-child pathologies emerge to embrace the family in destructive behavior patterns. The alcoholic may force the child into what family-systems theorists call double binds. The alcoholic wants the child to support his or her alcoholism through faulty reasoning such as, "My drinking really results from your mother's constant nagging of us." The child, of course, does not want to anger the alcoholic father nor to be put in opposition to the mother. No matter what the child does, he or she is unable to have a healthy relationship with either parent. The child, anxious over being put in an inappropriate and dysfunctional role, attempts to please both parties, thus establishing distrustful and insecure relationships with the parents. In effect, we have an unhealthy triangular relationship that promotes continuing stress (Kerr and Bowen 1988, Swick 1987).

At-risk families create perceptual contexts that represent real and imagined problems. For example, an unemployed father may imagine that his position in the family is lessened while family members actually empathize with his plight. In many cases perceptual orientations become distorted because fact and fantasy are not differentiated, often due to poor communication, inadequate problem-solving skills, and past family-reaction patterns. Dependency syndromes such as chemical addictions and combinations of other distortion processes also have a negative influence (Pittman 1987). Once a pattern of perceptual and/or behavioral distortion becomes internalized, individual and family energy is absorbed by these closed, recurrent, and destructive tendencies. Family members feel trapped by the very presence of seemingly unsolvable problems, thus adopting pessimistic and fate-filled responses to each others' lives as well as becoming dependent on the internalized ways of relating to each other (Kagan and Schlosberg 1989, Pittman 1987).

While all families struggle with relationship stressors, at-risk families are absorbed by such stress. Triangles exist in every family system. They provide a means by which individuals can develop balance in their lives. Most families, however, create enough balance in their relationships so that each person can differentiate his or her self in healthy ways. Families in risk situations often lose the viability that comes from individuation and become enmeshed in high-anxiety relationship patterns. Such emotionally charged relationships foster closed and rigid ways of dealing with stress. Instead of using relationships as a means of feedback and personal development, at-risk families tend to respond to each other in reactive, emotionally charged ways (Nichols 1988).

While parents may realize that they and their children are functioning in unhealthy ways, they may not see alternatives or the means by which they can change the situation. Case studies of children at risk indicate that in some cases the parents were aware of the risks present in the family's situation, but were lacking in ideas on how they could improve the environment. In one case, for example, a single-parent father who worked the night shift realized his son was staying up until midnight and that this pattern was causing the child to fall asleep during the day. When confronted with the school's concern during a conference, he explained that the child could not sleep until he arrived home from work—the child was too afraid to sleep. The father could not afford a "sitter," but he promised to try to improve the situation. This same father later explained to a social worker that he lacked the money to get his child into little league ball, but was fearful if his child was able to join the team that he might get hurt because of the crime in the neighborhood. He felt lucky, he said, because his child stayed in the house watching television and did not go on the streets where drugs were wild. This father certainly was caring, understood the risks he and his son faced, but lacked ideas and resources on how to cope with the problems (Frymier 1991).

In other cases, parents may not fully understand the risk factors confronting the family. When parents and children internalize abusive and/or destructive life styles, they come to see them as normal. In their minds it is other people who are abnormal and at risk, not them. Many teachers have been shocked to hear a parent say, "I told him to hit that child if he bothered him again. He must learn to fight for what is his!" Or, a parent may not see schooling as achievable or valuable for a child. As one parent said, "None of us is school material. He will have to make his way some other way." These comments reflect a perceptual orientation that is limited, punitive, and rigid. It is likely that such perceptions have been heavily influenced by context risks such as poverty, intergenerational abuse, and poor family and school experiences (Swick 1984, 1991b).

The key factor in supporting parent and family wellness is the nurturing in them of the potential for seeing positive alternatives in life (Sigel 1985). The reflective and proactive parent "sees" possibilities and options for family growth, having internalized a problem-solving approach to life. At-risk families, for various reasons, perceive their status quo as the only way to survive. The aggression, dependency, debilitating experiences, and distorted images of how to relate to each other have become so ingrained that other possibilities are indeed very threatening (Kagan and Schlosberg 1989, Kerr and Bowen 1988).

When people become dependent upon recurring problems to maintain their identity, change is feared until it can be seen as a positive force in their lives (Garbarino 1982). This is why early childhood intervention efforts must address the family's total system. For example, when an alcoholic parent enters a recovery program and gains control of the problem, the entire family must process this change. Past responses and interaction patterns of alcoholic families must be revised and

adjusted (Towers 1989a). Too often a fan,
of deeper social and emotional stress
relationship system. The family may use th
alcoholic parent, or the ill grandparent as a pi
the realities of pervasive family stress (Kerr an
is important to recognize that when families r
may be indicating their insecurity in dealing wi
Given that many high-risk families are isolated fro          ural
feedback systems present in the community, thei  igidity of
living is more a matter of inexperience than one of dysfunction.
The mother who fears putting her child in a child-development
program may be reflecting her ignorance of the value of this
service or her negative experiences with child-care programs. The
parent may also have become dependent on the daily rituals that
are a part of having the child at home. Losing the child to day
care may be a threat to her own identity (Powell 1989).

Changing our perceptions of ourselves and our relationships with others is embedded within the family-environment
system. Most people change their perceptions when they sense
the support to pursue the many actions that are required and
when they see the new events and behaviors as desirable. This
process is based upon some essential elements: an awareness that
existing perceptions are inadequate, the presence of supportive
others who have the trust of the person involved, the availability
of options that the person views as useful, the time-space
framework for negotiating the many nuances that comprise the
change process, and a cultural system that is accepting of the
person's goal of strengthening their life status (L'Abate 1990,
Sigel 1985).

At-risk families face more than the usual stress in
pursuing change. Consider the many possible barriers they
experience: negative experiences with change efforts in the past,
extremely limited resources to use in negotiating the elements of
the change process, low and/or negative social supports,
inadequate feelings about dealing with change, and various other
real and imagined barriers. These barriers are not unsurmounta-

families have some past success stories to cope with ...cular stress. In fact, research on early childhood prevention-projects indicate that when parents gain insight into the problem-solving process early, they integrate these perceptions and skills into their life style (Langer 1989, Schaefer 1991).

Family changes take place gradually and require a change in the way individual members perceive themselves, their environment, and what is important within the person-environment relationship. This process of altering how we perceive things requires support and encouragement, particularly when the change involves major adaptations in the family's way of life. Consider, for example, the mother who has never been to the pediatrician with her child. Many fears may precede her trying out this new pattern of living: What do I say to the pediatrician? What if the doctor finds something wrong with me or my child? Will they let me pay on a monthly basis? How will I be able to understand the doctor? These and other fears, while seemingly ridiculous to people who go to pediatricians regularly, are very serious concerns to the parent who has never experienced this process. With the appropriate support, we know that many parents can resolve their fears and come to value the many benefits of pediatric care.

With support from valued friends and helpers, families can negotiate the change process in a beneficial manner. In particular, first-time parents can seek out a confidant they trust, a person who will gently mentor them as they attempt to respond to the changes that come with family development. Many at-risk parents have never experienced the intimacy of trusting relationships and thus may need encouragement and guidance on how to create helping relationships (Fraiberg 1977).

There is considerable evidence that parents and families who have significant others as helpers accomplish many positive changes in life style. Hetherington (1979) found that single-parent mothers who had quality support persons were more proactive in relating and responding to family needs. Pence (1988) noted that parents and families who had access to high-resource contexts were more problem-solving oriented in their approach to life. In an ethnographic report, Swick (1992) observed that at-risk parents who had never participated in school activities came to value this process when they had a friend (in the form of a home-school worker) who guided them through the system and supported them in positive ways.

Without exception, all family change (regardless of which family member may be the primary focus) ultimately influences every aspect of the family system. Before any new behavior pattern can acquire its full power, it must become integrated into the family's cultural fabric (Kotre and Hall 1990). It must be perceived as integral to the family's belief system, seen as critical to its identity. This process of integration occurs over time and through having many favorable experiences where the new behavior leads to family benefits. This is true of any substantive change that families experience. The human learning system is such that our perceptions of how things work is more important than how they actually work. Realizing that health care, schooling, and other positive life activities are beneficial to our continued growth requires changes in our perceptions, values, and beliefs (Sigel 1985). For all of us, this process requires that we have helpers.

## RESPONDING POSITIVELY TO THE NEEDS OF AT-RISK FAMILIES

Being a helper is not as simple as the term may indicate. Indeed, many helpers have come away from the experience perplexed and dismayed. Early childhood educators are primary sources of help for families. As professionals and caring persons, it is important that we fully understand how to be positive helpers. There are particular insights from research that can guide our understanding of the helping process and strengthen our position as helpers.

A significant insight deals with the context of helping relationships. Context, in relation to helping, refers to the elements within the system of helping. It is known, for example, that people seeking help look for helpers who have similar context attributes; that is, they want help from someone who can empathize with their situation. This does not mean that helpers must have all the attributes of the people they are serving; that would be impossible. What it does mean is that helping relationships are more likely to have meaning when the people involved perceive that they have similar contexts regarding the need and situation being addressed (Spacapan and Oskamp 1992). For example, parents place their trust in care givers and teachers whom they perceive to have similar goals and beliefs (Galinsky 1987). Real and imagined disparities can emerge when families view their helpers as isolated from their context. This chasm between family and helpers can and does preclude meaningful relationships (Lightfoot 1978). Positive responses to the needs of families thus requires the building of context that provides those involved in helping relationships with a sense of mutual trust and empathy (Swick 1991b). This context building means that helpers have to acquire an understanding of the families they are working with in order to relate to their perceptions of reality. Swick (1991a, 1992) provides an example of how this context building can take place within early childhood education-settings. He describes how trained home-school workers used home visiting, small group discussions, and individualized parent-support activities to develop context similarities and trust relationships with parents of at-risk children. These home-school workers were from the community and were respected by most of the families they served, thus providing some initial context congruence between school and family. By focusing on the needs parents identified as crucial to their families, these helpers were able to create an empathetic atmosphere.

Closely related to context is the need for trust within the helping relationship. The insight that helping relationships are built on trust seems clear, yet research indicates that this element is especially crucial to the qualitative features of family life. Trust is a subjective faith that another person or group has one's interest at the core of action. As Erikson (1982) observes, trust is really faith in the consistent pattern of events and experiences that comprise what each of us perceives as meaningful in life. In seeking helpers, families look for people they can trust. The questions they ask as they seek helpers include: Does this person care about us? Is this person interested in our family beyond tomorrow? Is this person skilled in helping us with the particular areas for which we are seeking help? Does this person have integrity? While parents may not ask these questions in the literal sense, they do seek answers to them through their interactions with teachers and other helpers. They find answers to these questions through their experiences with helpers. For example, they watch how teachers relate to their children and to them. They observe how teachers relate to their needs, particularly with regard to how they treat them. Positive helping relationships require a continuing development of trust between families and their helpers (Galinsky 1990).

Trusting relationships include a sense of mutuality, a common perception that helpers and those being helped can and indeed do exchange roles and learn from each other (Erikson 1959). Reciprocity is at the center of growing relationships. In many cases at-risk families have rarely experienced reciprocity. Too often they have been encouraged to see themselves as powerless. Positive helpers need to nurture a sense of self-confidence in the families with which they work. This can occur in several ways: by inviting parents to help out in the classroom, by creating a mentoring system where experienced and successful parents help others, by involving parents in gradually taking on leadership roles, and through other tasks that support the building of autonomy in parents.

Within any viable relationship, autonomy of individual purpose and action is essential. Regardless of the risk conditions in which families function, the generation of individual and group power must be a primary mission of the helper (Spacapan and Oskamp 1992). In each person there is a desire to control at least a part of one's destiny. This desire to distinguish our identity is not extinguished when we are at risk, unless our relationships promote it. Research suggests that a major way to help at-risk families is to involve them in activities where they increase their control of life and acquire a sense of autonomy (Swick and Graves 1986). Helpers can accomplish this process by promoting self-reliance in families. This might begin in small ways, such as having parents plan a daily schedule for the family. Another activity is to involve children in making choices about their day's "work" and then having them review their achievements at the end of the day. In some situations it may be a case of helping parents relate to settings where they can acquire skills to organize their talents.

In all aspects of human interaction, open and honest communication is vital. This means that early childhood professionals need to be good listeners, positive and honest in their family-support efforts, and open to the ideas of parents and children regardless of their cultural or personal contexts. Studies on helping relationships indicate that a mutually responsive communication arrangement strengthens the entire process (Spacapan and Oskamp 1992). This is particularly so in cases where families are under heavy stress. This critical element can be nurtured through regular contacts with parents, by closely observing parent and child concerns, and by showing parents and children you are a person of integrity.

## Helping Behaviors for Effective Relationships with Families

These insights into being an effective helper can become the foundation of a caring profession. Are we persons that can be counted on when needed? Within reasonable human limits, are we honest, receptive to family concerns, and truly sensitive to familial needs for growth? Have we created an environment that invites reciprocity, promotes family autonomy, and is based on mutual respect for each other? The early childhood profession has historically been committed to these values as a process of

70

individual, family, and community growth. It is critical that we address these insights on helping in our work with at-risk families. In effect, we must ask ourselves as professionals if our efforts are indeed empowering families. The following are helpful reminders in this regard.

- Recognize the need for reciprocity in human relationships. From the very outset, create opportunities where families can contribute to the helping process. A sense of control is critical to the entire family.
- Be aware of what your motivation is in being in a helping role. Recognize the value of the helping role and develop a sense of trust in yourself and the people with whom you are working.
- Emphasize collaborative strategies where families are involved in developing plans that they see as beneficial to them. Collaboration helps to build mutuality and promotes a sense of power within the relationship system.
- Know your strengths and limits as a helper. Avoid trying to be all things in the relationship; that inevitably leads to disappointment and can eventually destroy the relationship. Identify and use other skilled and supportive helpers. Encourage mentoring, peer helping, and use of community resources to broaden your helping team.
- Recognize the systemic nature of helping situations. Balance your efforts within the family so that you have a comprehensive approach, involving everyone in activities that truly empower them. Create a sharing process where family members become each others' helpers.

The most consistent problem in helping relationships is a cultural insensitivity to the values and strengths that are present in the lives of families. Early childhood professionals take pride in having a history of being committed to the integrity of

71

families. We need to enrich this helping value by coming to know our parents and children in ways that strengthen their integrity.

A key strategy approach for helpers is to team with the family—to use their perspectives on needs, purpose, approach, and on the type of helping relationship that best suits the family. This teaming philosophy needs to serve as a foundation for all aspects of the relationship. Our goal is not to individually design educational and support activities for families but to engage family members as partners in the process of developing plans and strategies that best meet their needs as they see them. Naturally, as professionals, we will have ideas on needs that can strengthen the family. These professional perceptions should be integrated with the family's perspectives (Dunst, Trivette, and Deal 1988; Pence 1988).

Positive helpers look for and promote the strengths of the family. This is a perceptual strategy because it requires close observation of parent and child habits that may not be readily apparent. In too many cases, helpers are trained to look for family problems. A balanced perspective is needed with the focus being on positive attributes that families can use to build self-confidence. For example, in spite of poverty, many families maintain close and supportive relationships with each other. This strength can be nurtured and used to build other family skills (Hale-Benson 1986, Stinnett 1981).

Be proactive in your helping approach, use concrete and visible supports as a way of strengthening the family. At-risk families are often immune to verbal responses to their needs. Providing a parent with transportation to school to visit the classroom is more effective than talking about it. Providing parents with specific feedback on child achievements and offering particular materials they can use at home with the child can also be effective. Following up on a need that has been identified, such as helping the child or parent get needed health care, is another example of meaningful support. Wherever possible, these supportive activities should be carried out in

72

partnerships where parents are informed, involved, and nurtured to take the leadership in extending these activities past the immediate event (Swick 1991a).

An essential strategy for having a continuing relationship is to involve the family in initiating or reactivating problem-solving skills. There are many opportunities to achieve this: by inviting parents to identify ways that can help their child, by conferencing with parents on ways they can organize family-learning time, by providing parents and children with resources where they can initiate the problem-solving process, and by encouraging parents and children to work together in finding relationship activities that they enjoy. These types of autonomy-building activities need to evolve in the relationship between helpers and families in ways that strengthen their respect for each other (Cochran 1988).

Peer helping, mentoring, and parent-share groups are additional ways to nurture parent and family strengths. Powell (1989) noted that parents responded better to the help they received from other parents because they were able to relate to each other's context. As professionals we should capitalize on this process and encourage parents to help each other. Opportunities for parents and children to be in caring roles also lead to new images of themselves. Swick (1991b, 1992) observed that as parents progressed in their helping skills they often developed new plans for continuing their education, pursuing new job skills, and enriching the family's literacy habits. The following are strategy perspectives that support families.

- Be consistent in your relationship with the family. Provide continuing support that is positive and closely related to the family's needs.
- Use diverse materials, resources, and approaches in your work. At-risk families are not interested in what works for others; they are most sensitive to their realities.
- Communicate often and in ways that both support and

gently challenge families to grow and become positive about themselves.

- Relate and respond to the entire family system; avoid putting family members in conflict with other family members. One way to accomplish this is to involve everyone in a full discussion of any new events and activities.
- Provide the family with continuous feedback. This is particularly important with families in risk predicaments as they need messages that help them to see how the process is emerging.
- Refine your relationship as family needs change. Promote "the parent as leader" philosophy whenever and wherever possible.
- Promote equal relationships with the family. It is critical that parents and children see you as a person who is able to understand and interact with them in positive ways.

Proactive and supportive strategies are more powerful in promoting family wellness than abstract, negative-oriented relationship patterns. An empowerment design for supporting at-risk families calls for emphasis on self-image and family harmony.

## SUPPORTING AT-RISK FAMILIES: AN EMERGING PARADIGM

The shift toward a more dynamic view of the developing person has been under way at least since the time of Freud. As Thomas Kuhn (1970) explains, paradigm shifts are gradual, subtle, and yet very powerful in shaping the way people and cultures function. They involve a reconstruction process by which people come to see themselves and others in new ways. In terms of the work of early childhood professionals, new and emerging paradigms provide us with new perspectives on children and families, and our relationships with them. Indeed, these new world views help us to redefine our roles toward becoming more empathetic and empowering helpers.

Within any belief system, there are several premises that comprise a framework by which we can see the world in distinct ways. The empathetic-ecological paradigm of human development and learning has several such premises or new assumptions about life that can guide our work with at-risk families. Following are some basic family-empowerment premises.

- The individual's development and learning is significantly influenced by early childhood experiences (Erikson 1982).
- The individual's development and learning potential is rooted in person-environment context (Maslow 1959).
- The individual's match between needs and resources is a determining influence on development (Hunt 1961).
- The individual's social and emotional development occurs in a sequential manner, based upon the security established in the trust relationship (Erikson 1982).
- The individual's learning and development is best facilitated through experiential involvement with real-life events (Dewey 1916).
- The individual's learning and development occurs in a constructivist manner (Piaget 1954).
- The individual's learning and development takes place within a nest of interlocking systems of human ecologies (Bronfenbrenner 1979).
- The individual's development is most vulnerable to positive and negative influences during the earliest years of life (Fraiberg 1977).
- The individual's social and emotional development is the primary result of the family-relationship system (Kerr and Bowen 1988).
- The individual's development and learning is best realized in environments where events and experiences are predictable, nurturing, and progressively challeng-

ing (Bronfenbrenner 1979).

These premises provide a foundation upon which a new paradigm for working with at-risk families can be actualized. With the knowledge that families function in interactive ways, early childhood professionals must shape their helping philosophy in directions that have a positive influence on the family. In this sense, no parent or family must ever be viewed as hopeless or even as less than vital to the community. No child, parent, or family must ever be viewed as unreachable or as incapable of learning and growing (Swick 1987).

With research that supports the construct that all healthy individuals can reach at least much of their human potential when needs and resources are in some type of balance, there is no valid excuse for using exclusionary, rigid, or demeaning practices with families (Galinsky 1990). The perspective that families need healthy contexts both within their relationships and in their linkages with the community includes us as helping professionals. It means that healthy environments begin with the way we see families, that our perceptions take into account their strengths (even the hidden strengths) and their situation.

A major part of this process is in our constructing a partnership vision of how the empowerment approach works to the advantage of everyone in the human community. With a progressive image of the family as a learning system, the emphasis shifts from deficit approaches to proactive, nurturing modes of relating to families. Family risks are not seen as problems of an individual, a specific family, or of a particular group of people. Rather, they are seen as weaknesses that have evolved in the entire human development process. Further, the emphasis shifts from focusing mainly on the risk factors to focusing on creating structures and relationships that nurture the person, family, and community toward healthier ways of living (Kessler, Goldston, and Joffe 1992).

The old paradigm was symbolized by treatment plans, professional domination, cause-effect thinking, and limited outcomes. In effect, it functioned on premises that saw the child and family in trouble, not the surrounding social system. Further, it looked for weakness, problems, and solutions directed toward specific issues. While this approach did accomplish some good for families, it rarely achieved the longer range goal of changing the assumptions and structure upon which families operate. An ecological/empathetic approach to working with families aims to empower, to develop a more positive and potent sense of self. It recognizes the connectedness of families to the community, and it seeks to engage all of the human partners in seeking healthier ways of living. As Stark (1992, pp. 170-71) states:

> If we ask about situations causing scarcity and lack of resources, making life hard for people or preventing the enhancement of their potential, we are not only asking about what is, but also for the causes and the background. And, most important we start a process without controlling the outcome.

A major part of empowering is linking up those who are powerless with the structure of power in the community. Before this can happen, early childhood professionals must have a sense of the strength and potential in the families with whom they work. A sense of partnership must be present in the professional-parent relationship.

While there are no rigidly defined steps to follow in using an empowerment approach to supporting at-risk families, there are guidelines that can be used as directions for truly strengthening families and children.

Observation of more than surface issues and behaviors is one direction that early childhood professionals need to pursue (Swick 1987). Coming to understand the strengths of all families regardless of the risks they face is critical to adopting an empowerment belief-system. How many people feel mistreated because they are not fully understood? In a fast-paced culture such as ours, people tend to see what they have been educated to

77

see. Learning to become a sensitive observer; looking for more than problems, needs, and causes; attempting to realize the person's strengths and the family's complete situation is essential (Kagan and Schlosberg 1989).

Perhaps the greatest barrier to becoming a truly responsive helper is our instinctive feeling of directing the arena in which children and families live. After all, most of us have been trained to teach thinking that we should prescribe a solution or mode of living that will help others. Truly empowering teachers are cognizant that listening is the bridge to new knowledge and values (Stark 1992). Research on the helping process indicates that when people are looking for help, they seek out someone who is willing to listen to their message (Spacapan and Oskamp 1992). Unfortunately, most people listen according to their predetermined conceptions of what a person or family needs. For example, Swick (1991b) noted that in a home-visiting program the visitors mistakenly thought parents wanted money for themselves as a part of their participation when what the parents were really trying to explain was their need for some way to pay for child care while they were attending group meetings.

Another dimension of this need for sensitive listening involves the helper in opening up to the verbal and nonverbal signals of children and families. This process certainly involves us in learning about the cultural and social perspectives of young families. What are the predominant values and strengths of families? What are the needs of the children and families through their views? Family behaviors only come to the surface when a truly responsive environment exists. Too often as professionals we assume that we know what families need. Yet these conceptions are usually limited and tainted by our own cultural experiences. Powell (1988), for example, explains how parent educators in a program designed to support at-risk parents became upset that the parents seemed more interested in talking with each other than in the formal parent-education content being offered. Through observation and an active-listening process, Powell found out that what parents were expressing was that the need for interpersonal contact with other parents was stronger than was the need for parenting information. Through communication between the parents and the parent educators, the two processes (interpersonal development and parenting information) were blended into a meaningful program.

Another direction that is integral to empowering children and families is the creation of "power structures" in which human services are connected in meaningful and accessible ways (Albee 1992). On the surface, this may appear to be an impossible challenge. Yet, if we conceptualize this as a process by which early childhood professionals seek out ways to relate school and family to the community system, it is a very achievable goal. A distinct attribute of most at-risk families is their isolation from the sources of power that are present in the community. Their most likely contacts with power sources come through their interaction with early childhood programs, churches, friends, and possibly a few support agencies.

Empowerment studies articulate the need for involving families in experiences where they shape significant parts of their destiny (Albee, Bond, and Monsey 1992; Comer and Haynes 1991; Pence 1988). By necessity, this involves people in reframing their images of themselves, creating images that project self-confidence and the self-discipline that is needed to pursue difficult challenges. It also often requires early childhood professionals to reframe their perceptions of parents and children, particularly as related to at-risk families. We rarely involve people who we lack confidence in, and people who see themselves as less than capable rarely risk the challenges of involvement.

Some of the more notable indicators of family-school involvement programs that have achieved some success in promoting parent-family integrity include:

- the presence of sensitivity among both parents and professionals to each other's specific needs,
- the use of continuous open and responsive communi-

cation between the family and the school,

- the presence of an attitude of going beyond the expected in helping and supporting each other,
- the use of decision-making processes that are truly responsive to the unique needs of the family and the school, and
- the presence of a system that supports and encourages family-strengthening activities.

The substance of an empowerment process is what makes for healthy families. An ecology for successful living is inclusive of all of the elements that support good beginnings for children and families. As helping professionals, we need to recognize and pursue a human agenda that assures all children and families a healthy start in life. Our focus must be comprehensive, yet responsive to the unique needs of each family.

A first step in this agenda to empower children and families is to assure that health and wellness are provided (The Report of the National Task Force on School Readiness 1991). This direction needs to include:

- prenatal care for all women,
- community awareness on the importance of prenatal care and family health, and
- nutrition and health programs.

Family wellness must also be addressed through community approaches that encourage parents and children to establish loving relationships. Families of all backgrounds are confronting high stress as they begin the family journey. Parent-education and family-wellness resource programs should be available for all families (Boyer 1991). Preventive practices such as the following need to be integrated into each community's social structure.

- education for family helpers of all disciplines that promotes family-prevention, family-friendly early childhood approach
- parent education that focuses on the critical emotional

and social needs of young families
- parent training and support for families with special needs in the areas of literacy, network building, health, child care, and related need areas
- family preservation strategies that identify and intervene at the earliest point possible in the family's development
- parent/family mental health centers that promote positive life styles (These should include services such as: family time-out, crisis counseling, preventive therapeutic services, and continuing education through community-wide efforts.)
- family-support services that enable parents and children to become involved in school and community activities. (Services might include: transportation, family-friendly visitors, emergency leave-time, and similar practices.)

Child-care and related quality early childhood education-programs are of special significance within the empowerment paradigm. They provide a context that can engender many services that strengthen children and families. These include: offering developmental screening, educating parents on literacy habits, identifying and addressing special family needs, and involving children and parents in enjoyable and meaningful learning experiences. Well-planned and comprehensive programs can strengthen children and parents in this early and critical part of their journey. These programs should promote total family involvement, supporting and promoting parental leadership in every way possible (Swick 1991b).

Literacy, job training, and related adult-education strategies are an integral part of family empowerment. An ecology of family wellness includes the vitality of parents. Their continuing growth as adults is highly related to their family leadership. As family advocates we can pursue literacy-promoting strategies, such as assuring that all young adults complete high school, engaging parents in acquiring the skills needed for life-long learning, and supporting parents in achieving meaningful career goals (Schorr and Schorr 1988).

A priority of the early childhood profession must be to begin the process of creating an empowered citizenry. This goal is only possible when the experiences of young children and their parents are indeed empowering. Sadly, over one-third of the nation's children arrive at school lacking in the needed resources to fully benefit from it. Further, many early childhood programs are not ready to engage in meaningful and success-oriented practices with young at-risk children. Many current school practices act as barriers to children's successful learning and development (Thompson and Hupp 1992).

More supportive practices are needed to promote a success orientation in children and families. These practices must be embedded within caring communities that "encourage public, private, and voluntary efforts to support young children and families before they arrive at school and once they reach the schoolhouse door " (Schultz and Lombardi 1992, p. 8). In particular, communities must address the debilitating circumstances that poor, single-parent families confront. There are strategies that all citizens can pursue: provide needed support resources so that teen-parents can complete school; develop peer self-help projects where parents help each other; support male mentoring activities for fatherless children; create enticements for divorced fathers to stay involved with the family; and establish family support centers in churches and other community groups (Boyer 1991, Pence 1988).

*Elements of Empowering Communities*

An empowerment paradigm can be realized through our individual efforts to pursue caring communities. This process calls for having the following elements.

- an ecological focus that is based on the premise that all families are powerful

- community and family-centered practices that place priority on the prevention of at-risk family contexts
- professional, legislative, and agency governing structures and policies that promote preventive, interdisciplinary, and family-intensive practices
- school-based programs that are responsive and supportive in relating to the needs of at-risk children and families.

## Individual Family Empowerment Strategies

Early childhood educators can provide the leadership for promoting the family empowerment philosophy through their sensitive and supportive work with parents and children. Our history has been one of pursuing this effort. Our profession, more than any other, advocates collaborative, equal, and proactive relationships with families. The following are directions each early childhood educator can pursue to foster stronger families.

- Nurture in ourselves a strong image of being a truly sensitive helping professional.
- Develop a positive vision of what each family can become within a society that values and supports families.
- Create family-program systems that promote more equitable and collaborative relationships with families.
- Develop insights and perspectives regarding families that place priority on their strengths and their potential as opposed to their weaknesses.
- Provide a system for continually nurturing professional-family relationships that foster high regard and cooperative action.
- Create program activities that invite parents and children to be the leaders in the family-school relationship.
- Foster warm, supportive, and positive parent-child relationships through modeling these behaviors with

parents and children.

- Organize family-support services within the school and with other agencies and groups that address the many stressors that face families.

Ultimately, an empowerment philosophy can be actualized within family relationships when parents and children have both a context and the vision for shaping sensitive and caring relationships. In a complex and often threatening social structure such as ours, families need support in building that needed context and in acquiring ideas on the needed vision. Our job is to be that support group.

Chapter 3

# UNDERSTANDING THE BARRIERS TO EMPOWERMENT

"At risk" is not a condition or situation experienced only by minority segments of the population; it is a set of barriers to empowerment that can influence any family. This chapter examines the various barriers to empowerment in families (and within family-school-community relationships) during the early childhood years. These include traditional barriers, social and economic barriers, sociocultural risks and opportunities, family dynamics, and even involvement of family helpers. The chapter also discusses attributes of "family health" and their relation to the empowerment process. It then explores new perspectives on supporting families in removing and/or overcoming barriers to their healthy functioning.

## TRADITIONAL BARRIERS TO FAMILY EMPOWERMENT

Several barriers have traditionally blocked child and family empowerment during the early childhood years.

### Isolation

The most consistent barrier is isolation from the environment (Swick 1987). This barrier is present in the relationships of at-risk families in multiple ways: in their lack of involvement in essential health services, in economic seclusion, in poor networking with other parents and families, and in poor or little involvement with early childhood professionals. In some cases, these forms of isolation are the result of poverty, illiteracy, and intergenerational values that reinforce an isolationist life-style (Edelman 1987). However, family isolation is also the result of negative (and in some cases, destructive) attitudes and behaviors on the part of professional helpers. A case in point is the often negative, nonsupportive family-school relationship pattern that emerges during the family's development in the early childhood years.

## Parent-Professional Relationships

Parent-professional relationships have often been counterproductive and negative (Gallagher, Beckman, and Cross 1983). Vague, limited, and professionally dominated relationship strategies have often discouraged parents from joining in partnership efforts (Graves and Gargiulo 1989). In effect, early childhood teachers have often unknowingly limited the role of parents to passive participation within a very confined system of conferences and group meetings (Gargiulo 1985). This has been especially evident in the minimal role that at-risk parents have played in family-school activities. Given the heavy demands of teaching, too often teachers have limited their role to classroom tasks and have viewed parental participation as a nuisance rather than as an empowerment opportunity (Seligman 1979). Evolving from this passive relationship pattern have been many negative family-school outcomes of which the most damaging has been the reinforcement in parents of an isolationist life-style.

Consequently, parents (particularly those in at-risk situations) have tended to view the school as a barrier to their family's development. For example, with regard to parental views of parent-professional relationships involving special needs children, Gargiulo (1985, p. 6) states:

> They have judged professionals to be insensitive, offensive, and incapable of understanding their situation because professionals themselves are rarely parents of an exceptional child.

Clearly, some teachers and other family helpers are sensitive and responsive to parent and family needs, yet far too often at-risk families feel they are not treated as equals. Thus, a key barrier to parental and family strengthening has often resided in the professional's skills (or lack of) for effectively relating to the needs of at-risk families. The ecological-empathetic perspective emphasizes the need for positive and equal parent-teacher relationships.

## Communication Skills

Poor or nonexistent communication skills have also been a major constraint in the lives of at-risk families (Kagan and Schlosberg 1989).

Within family relationships the prevailing mode of interaction is often one of blaming, defensiveness, verbal reprimands, and limited explanation. Often, this pattern of communication has been acquired within an intergenerational system of abuse. Complicating the communication context of at-risk families is the inadequate preparation of professionals for relating to them in proactive ways (Swick 1984). The traditional professional paradigm in most of the helping professions has been a limited and inadequate structure for helping families acquire competency in relating to the school and community (Schaefer 1991).

Ineffective communication between parents and schools also impedes the functioning of many at-risk parents and children. Given the heavy demands of teachers and school officials, and the busy lives of parents, communication is often slighted and used only when a crisis occurs. When there has been little time for building effective communicative relationships, however, crises seem to spur negative interactions, and consequently, counterproductive relationships (Bigner 1985, Carkuff and Anthony 1979). Poor problem-solving skills often emerge from settings and relationships where thought and anticipatory planning are lacking. At-risk families traditionally confront situations where problem-solving requirements are high and resources needed for carrying out such conflict resolution are low (Swick 1987). Studies of internal and external family relationships indicate "at risk" is further complicated by this lack of problem-solving ability.

## Conception of "At Risk"

More than anything, the traditional negative and myopic understanding of being "at risk" in our culture has been the major barrier to our full empowerment as families, citizens, and professionals (Albee 1992). Typically, the term "at risk" is equated with "less than," "damaged," and other negative images. Professionals have often viewed "at risk" as equivalent with failure or little potential to achieve. Tragically, parents and children quickly internalize this message and behave in ways that reinforce a cycle of nonproductive behaviors. Low or negative self-image evolves from such poor and inadequate conceptions of what it means to be at risk.

Schools and social support agencies have suffered the most from adopting this erroneous conception. Tracking, punitive discipline, low expectations, and unequal treatment of children and parents are some of the most damaging practices (Galinsky 1990). Derogatory practices such as making at-risk parents wait longer than others for basic services, treating them with less dignity, lecturing to them in punitive ways, and focusing on their weaknesses to the extreme are practices that have prevailed when a traditional paradigm has been adopted (Kagan and Schlosberg 1989).

## SOCIAL AND ECONOMIC BARRIERS

Interrelated with these traditional barriers to family empowerment are multiple social and economic barriers. These include poverty, the drug-abuse epidemic, inadequate early childhood care, illiteracy, excessive teen birth-rates, homelessness, AIDS, poor health care, malnutrition, and other debilitating conditions. In effect, the social and economic infrastructure of parenting and family life is at risk (Hamburg 1992).

Earlier in the book we briefly examined the key risk areas prevalent in the lives of children and families during the early childhood years. The potential harm to families was considered. Here, the focus is on the actual "barrier influence" these risks have when they become pervasive parts of the lives of parents and children. Sadly, these "barriers" are forming a cancer on our social and cultural future. We are at risk as a society when families experience these barriers to the extreme degrees they are today.

*Poverty*

Traditionally, poverty has been one of the most persistent barriers to childhood health. In the past, however, poverty had boundaries in which particular indicators could be targeted and addressed by caring adults and communities (Hamburg 1992). What is becoming identified as the "New Poverty" is more multifaceted, intense, complex, and less adaptable within eroding community-support structures. The following are the realities of the poverty barrier as it currently influences the lives of young children and families (Children's Defense Fund 1990, Gibbs 1990, Hamburg 1992).

- One out of four children under six years of age in America lives in poverty.
- Support programs for children under six years of age have decreased four percent, while supports for adults over the age of 50 have increased 52 percent.
- Families with children under six years of age are now the "poorest of the poor" and are more likely to lack basic health insurance than any other segment of the population.

The penetration of poverty into the family's total system is seen in many ways. Perhaps the most alarming factor is the absence of the family's "community net" that once protected parents and children from the full force of poverty (Edelman 1992). With increased economic demands and fewer support systems available to parents to use in buffering children from poverty's negative power, many poverty-related barriers have emerged to complicate the situation.

- Four percent of all children three to six years old care for themselves while their mothers work (Children's Defense Fund 1988).
- Every 36 minutes a child is killed or injured by a gun. Children more than any other age group are prone to injuries in the home (Gibbs 1990).
- More than two million children were reported abused, neglected, or both in 1987 alone (Children's Defense Fund 1990).
- Poor children are more likely to be born in less than supportive health settings and to receive low quality health care during the first year of life (Gibbs 1990).
- In 1989 alone, 11 percent of all babies born in America had some trace of drugs. The numbers are higher than they were in 1985 (Viadero 1989).

The decreasing safety and security net that many children and parents used to buffer poverty in the past is extending the negative influence of this barrier. Crime, drugs, poor health care, and related stressors are found in poor family contexts more often than in other family settings (Schorr and Schorr 1988).

## Chemical Abuse

The most insidious barrier to the full empowerment of children and families is drug abuse. This barrier can have the immediate effect of permanently damaging the child (and certainly degrading the parent, too) as well as long-term medical, social, emotional, and educational effects. The "drug epidemic" in our society has become a major barrier to everyone's healthy functioning. Newman and Buka (1991, pp. 27-23) document the severity of this barrier as it is emerging within young families.

Some 40,000 children a year are born with learning

impairments related to their mother's alcohol use. Drug abuse during pregnancy affects 11 percent of newborns each year—more than 425,000 infants in 1988. Some 260,000 children each year are born at below normal weights—often because they were prenatally exposed to nicotine, alcohol, or illegal drugs.

Chemical abuse syndromes are prevalent in every socioeconomic group and occur in epidemic proportion in poor, minority populations. The syndromes take on different forms (e.g., alcohol abuse, cocaine addiction, smoking during pregnancy), and yet show great consistency in the types of negative influences they have on children, parents, and indeed the entire society.

In the most severe cases, death or permanent damage is done to the child. Cocaine, for example, can cause miscarriage, intrauterine death, and premature birth. Alcohol can also cause these same problems. For the children who do survive, the degree of damage to their system varies; for some the damage is permanent and massive. Fontana (1992, p. 35) highlights the tragic impact cocaine has on many children:

Mothers' use of cocaine during pregnancy can cause even more frightful damage to babies in the womb: deformed hearts and lungs, abnormal genital and intestinal organs, permanent neurological impairment, paralysis, seizures, strokes, and irrevocable brain damage. Some of these babies are born literally without a brain. At the very least, cocaine babies come into the world undersized and addicted, suffering the terrible agony of cocaine withdrawal. And they do suffer terribly.

For the children who are resilient enough to survive these early effects of chemical poisoning, there are many debilitating barriers that confront them throughout life. Burgess and Streissguth (1992, pp. 24-25) identify some of the key characteristics of Fetal Alcohol Syndrome children as follows:

- small in physical stature
- easily excitable, extremely active
- inattentive restlessness
- poor in language/communication skills
- impulsive, low attention span
- ineffective problem-solving skills
- antisocial behavior tendencies
- poor academic performance.

As Griffith points out, drug-exposed children can be helped through effective early intervention, particularly through interventions that target social competency and language/communication skills. Yet, he also notes that children affected by drug exposure are likely to have continuing difficulties with sensitivity to hyperactivity and with language and communication skills. The key difficulty is that in too many cases drug-exposed infants and children also experience other debilitating environmental conditions. Hutchinson (1991, p. 32) notes:

> The combined effects of prenatal drug exposure with a home environment that provides little or no nurturance, understanding, or support for the child create a terrible challenge to the teachers. But initial experimental programs suggest that these children can benefit greatly from placement in highly structured, highly tailored educational day-care settings beginning in early infancy.

The reality is, however, that too few children receive these high quality experiences. Likewise, in far too many cases drug-abusing mothers are not receiving the essential counseling, rehabilitation, and support services needed for them to create a nurturing family environment (Fontana 1992). The ultimate tragedy with the chemical-dependence barrier is that it is totally preventable. Through education, counseling, and community-empowerment strategies, this risk factor is manageable.

## Poor Early Childhood Care

The quality of children's early experiences is now accepted as a major influence on their lifelong patterns of social and educational functioning (Boyer 1991). Ironically, at the same time that the importance of the early years has been recognized as critical to development, the care and early learning environments of young children have deteriorated in quality. It is estimated that less than 30 percent of poor children are served by even minimally adequate early childhood programs (Boyer 1991). And even these children often experience very low-quality care in programs that are poorly supported. The problem of poor care is not restricted to poor children; it is prevalent in every social and economic group in the society (Brophy 1986). It also reaches beyond "out-of-home" care settings in that many home environments lack the nurturance and security so essential to children's healthy development and learning. As Brophy notes (1986, p. 58):

> What the late child psychologist Selma Fraiberg called "the magic years" don't seem so magical anymore. Whether they come from cities, suburbs, or farms; stable families or broken homes; kids today must cope with a world in which both parents work, in which sex and drugs cloud even the elementary-school yard, and in which violence is only as far away as the living-room television screen.

Clearly, the most alarming barrier to the development of children and parents is the marked decline in the quantity and quality of adult-child relationships. David Hamburg (1992, p. 8) says it well:

> The change in the frequency and quality of contact between children and their adult relatives is remarkable. Not only are mothers home much less, but, as mentioned, there is little if any evidence that fathers are spending more time at home to compensate. Only about five percent of American children

see a grandparent regularly, a much lower level than in the past.

In terms of care within the home and in out-of-home care and education settings, young children (and their parents) are likely to experience settings in which the following attributes prevail.

- poorly trained staff
- inadequate adult-child relationships
- unsafe physical settings
- punitive adult-child interactions
- poorly equipped environments
- passive, uninteresting learning experiences

Poor quality early childhood care leads to multiple problems for children and families. Typically, children who experience little meaningful learning during this period of development fail to develop the skills needed for later school and life participation. These skills include persistence in task completion, cooperation with others, empathy and affective behaviors, creativity, self-confidence and self-reliance, language and communication skills, good health/physical development, and positive emotional and spiritual processes (Tobin, Wu, and Davidson 1989). Likewise, family functioning is negatively influenced by poor quality early childhood care. Parents report more stress with regard to their role as guide and protector when their children are in unsafe and/or insecure child care. They also exhibit less confidence in themselves as parents, exhibit more job stress, and tend to be more pessimistic with their children (Schaefer 1991).

In spite of the small gains achieved through the passage of the Act for Better Child Care, millions of children and families are floundering in poor home and out-of-home care and learning settings. Poor quality early care remains a subtle, yet powerful, barrier to the full empowerment of our society.

## Illiteracy

It is indeed a national tragedy that in one of the wealthiest democracies of the world many citizens lack the literacy skills to effectively participate in its social and economic activities. More than 23 million adults are functionally illiterate; 13 percent of all teenagers join this group annually (Cooperative Extension System 1989). In addition, the school dropout rates exceed 50 percent in many of the nation's urban centers; the national average is approximately 25 percent (Doyle 1989). Illiteracy is a functional barrier within the lives of parents and children. It precludes the growth that is essential to healthy family development. Parents lack the educational skills to join the economic and social system needed for family sustenance, and children lack role models who can provide them with the needed guidance toward becoming integrated into the meaningful work of society.

Undereducated and/or illiterate adults make for poor parents in that they are unable to articulate their caring and compassion for children in fully productive ways. Hewlett (1991, pp. 264-274) identifies the following attributes that are prevalent in families where illiteracy is a continuing barrier.

- poor communication patterns
- underemployment/chronic unemloyment
- chronic social pathologies (abuse, drug abuse, criminal behavior)
- isolation from social and educational activities
- negative/punitive family interactions

Illiteracy establishes a foundation for intergenerational dysfunction within the family and society. It is a debilitating barrier that might be called the self-inflicted drug that leads to chemical, social, and emotional pathologies. It is a barrier that we can remove through meaningful social investment. Hewlett (1991, p. 270) summarizes the tragedy of this barrier as related to our social values:

In the 1980s we more than doubled the amount of money we spent on prisons, while slashing programs that underpin poor children—housing, subsidies, Pell grants, and measles vaccinations were all cut back. This type of short-sighted economy will undoubtedly feed our surging crime rate into the future. It is no coincidence that more than 80 percent of inmates in state prisons are high school dropouts, and most can't read and write well enough to fill out an application form, much less hold down a paying job. Crime is easy when you have nothing to do.

## Teen Births

The epidemic of teenage births during the 1980s has created a "nest" of barriers: more health problems, lower incomes, increased family stress, and the potential for many additional difficulties. The U.S. Department of Health and Human Services (1992, p. 11) states:

Maternal age is a risk factor at both ends of the childbearing years: under age 17 and over age 40. Teenage women, more than a million of whom become pregnant each year in the United States, are at particular risk of having low-birth weight babies.

Both child and parent are negatively influenced by teen births as noted in the report (U.S. Department of Health and Human Services 1992, p. 18). According to the report, teen mothers are more likely to

- not finish high school,
- be unemployed,
- have low-birth-weight babies, and
- lack effective parenting skills.

There are additional risks that appear more often among teens who are pregnant. Magid and McKelvey (1987) note that teen parents are more likely to have a child that dies in the first year of life. This is due to the lack of prenatal care among most pregnant teens. Teen parents are also more likely to be unmarried and to lack a viable support system. It appears that in many cases, teen parenthood is a continuation of an intergenerational cycle of early marriage, poverty, inadequate education, and consequent unemployment. Magid and McKelvey (1987) note that the Guttmacher Institute's report on "Teenage Pregnancy" indicates that 82 percent of girls who give birth at age 15 or younger are the daughters of teenage mothers. They go on to note (p. 163):

> The impact of teenage pregnancies is not just with the young mothers. In addition to being at risk psychologically, the babies of teenagers are at much higher risk medically; the infant death-rate is 200 percent higher among babies born to teenagers than to those born to women in their twenties.
>
> The problems faced by children of teen parents begin before these children are born. Only one in five girls under age 15 receives any prenatal care during the first three months of pregnancy. The combination of poor medical care and poor diet also contributes to problems during pregnancy. Teens are 92 percent more likely to have anemia and 23 percent more likely to have premature babies.

The long-term impact of this barrier is tragic on child, family, and society. For example, teen mothers drop out of school at an alarming rate. Only half of those who give birth before 18 complete high school. Compare that with the 96 percent of those who postpone childbirth (Magid and McKelvey 1987, p. 165). Further, they are likely to earn less than half of what others make who postpone childbirth until their twenties. They are also more likely to be single parents and to experience extreme family dysfunction.

As a society (and particularly as early childhood professionals) we can and must address this barrier through preventive sex and family education, social support programs, and literacy and job-training efforts. To ignore this barrier is to condemn a significant part of our population to a poor quality of life. Magid and McKelvey (1987, p. 171) summarize the problem well:

> When a child is forced into motherhood too soon, the losses range from monetary to emotional for both her and her child. As we noted, these are often the babies who suffer the most from lack of bonding.

## Homelessness

Home is where children and adults identify with particular stabilizing forces as well as create indications of their identity. While this process is always critical, it is of absolute necessity for children and parents as they develop both their individual and family identity. Thus, the growing problem of homeless families is a barrier to the empowerment of children and parents. In 1985 families accounted for 27 percent of the homeless population; by 1990 that figure had risen to 34 percent. In 1990 the demand for shelter for families in major cities increased by an average of 17 percent over the 1989 level, with some cities reporting increases of 60 percent (Linehan 1992). While homelessness is most visible in cities, it is prevalent in rural areas, small towns, and in suburbs (Wright 1989).

By most calculations women and young children account for about one-third of homeless people; this is in contrast to the early 1980s when only about one-tenth were young families (Wright 1989). While it is difficult to estimate, most accounts suggest that on any given night there are about one million homeless children in the United States. This figure does not include the "hidden homeless" who are not officially counted in the statistics. They often survive by moving from "relative to relative or friend" until they are forced into shelters or other living arrangements. In effect, they do not have a home of their own. Indeed, there are likely two million homeless children when "temporary living arrangements" are included.

Parents and children in homeless situations face particular constraints: they are constantly moving, experience frequent change of schools and friends, live in overcrowded (and often unsafe) conditions, lack access to basic human resources, and lack a consistent nurturing support system (Towers 1989b). Add these constraints to the fact that most homeless families are headed by a poor, single-parent mother, and the realities of this barrier are very evident. The following are particular stressors these parents and children confront. It is important to keep in mind that each child and parent responds to these stressors differently. It is also critical to keep in mind that these barriers are manageable when society provides adequate family supports as a universal part of basic family programs. In other words, the following constraints are indeed manageable as is indicated by programs that have successfully enabled families to achieve the security of acquiring and maintaining an identity within more permanent housing (Linehan 1992).

- constant mobility, lack of stable setting
- lack of space for personal identity items
- constantly questioned by official authorities on motives
- lack of a sense of "community"
- constant fear of authority figures like teachers
- lack of access to basic human services
- consistent problems with transportation
- intense sense of loss due to lack of home address
- consistent negative self-image feedback

Homelessness further complicates the poverty and related stress of young families. Parents experience constant difficulties getting mail, accessing services that require a "permanent address," and obtaining employment. The term "homeless" brings with it an identification of instability in the eyes of employers and professionals. Children feel frustrated because they lack "private space," are viewed in stereotypical ways by teachers, are often moved just when they attain some positive

99

friendships, and because of family problems related to homelessness (Towers 1989b). Early childhood programs and staff can lead the way in helping families attain a sense of family within the program's context and by promoting community action that provides quality housing and living conditions for all families.

*AIDS*

HIV (Human Immunodeficiency Virus) is an insidious but preventable barrier that is currently causing tremendous damage in the lives of infected parents and children. HIV-infected parents and children stand the chance of getting AIDS (Acquired Immunodeficiency Syndrome). HIV and AIDS are highly interrelated with drug abuse and unsafe sex. In November 1991, the Centers for Disease Control (CDC) reported 3,246 cases of AIDS among children under the age of 13. This number does not accurately reflect the number of children with HIV infection and thus undercounts the children needing special services (Seidel 1992). For every person who has AIDS, there are several others who are infected with the HIV virus. HIV has become the greatest infectious cause of pediatric mental retardation in the United States (U.S. Department of Health and Human Services 1992). Women and infants are among the populations where HIV and AIDS are increasing the fastest. This devastating virus occurs in disproportionate numbers in low-income, minority families. Children acquire the virus from maternal transmission.

HIV-infected children exhibit several developmental delays and problems. These delays and problems are often caused by HIV and related causes, such as genetic factors, poor prenatal care, substance abuse by parents, low birth weight, nutritional deficits, and environmental trauma (Seidel 1992). The unique feature of HIV in children is the progressive deterioration of the central nervous system. It is this deterioration that causes the multiple developmental problems that children experience. Seidel (1992, p. 39) explains:

100

It is not usually the compromised health associated with HIV infection that causes developmental delay; instead, the neurotoxic influence of HIV causes brain damage that results in a loss of previously attained developmental milestones.

The following are HIV-related developmental disabilities that most often occur in infected children.

- gross and fine motor skill deficits
- cognitive impairments
- language delays
- emotional/behavioral problems

HIV and AIDS present barriers not only to children and their parents but to the entire community. This is a clearly preventable barrier, one that can be influenced through education and continuing community awareness in the areas of safe sex and drug-abuse prevention (Seidel 1992). Further, early childhood professionals need to prepare environments that are as barrier free as possible for children with HIV and AIDS. Intensive family-support efforts can and are influencing children and parents in positive and empowering ways.

## Poor Health Care

An almost totally preventable barrier to child and parent dysfunction, poor health care emerges where ignorance and inadequate health supports are most prevalent. Yet, this syndrome is not restricted to the poor; it is a growing barrier within family ecologies in every social and economic group (U.S. Department of Health and Human Services 1992). The lack of a national policy on child and family health-services only increases the "risk" of more family-related health problems, particularly among very young families. The "crisis" in health care for children and parents reaches every aspect of family wellness. Injuries, poor prenatal care, grossly inadequate health insurance systems, and the dramatic rise in children's mental health problems are simply the surface problems of a nation's neglect (Gibbs 1990). The irony and tragedy of the nation's poor health-care system is represented in the following example (Gibbs 1990, p. 43).

> Fully 250,000 babies are born seriously underweight each year. To keep these infants in intensive care costs about $3,000 a day, and these babies are two to three times more likely to be blind, deaf, or mentally retarded. On the other hand, regular checkups and monitoring of a pregnant woman can cost as little as $500 and greatly increase the chances that she will give birth to a healthy baby.

Low birth weight is associated with various debilitating conditions: early death, persistent childhood illnesses, poor school performance, and family dysfunction. It negatively affects child, parent, and society. The tragedy is that this barrier is preventable. The following excerpts from the Healthy People 2000 Report (U.S. Department of Health and Human Services 1992, p. 12) reveals the potential that exists in proper prenatal care.

> Numerous studies have demonstrated that early and comprehensive prenatal care reduces rates of infant death and low birth weight. An expectant mother with no prenatal care is three times as likely to have a low-birth-weight baby. The effect of early prenatal care is especially evident in studies of high-risk groups, such as adolescents and poor women.
>
> Prenatal care can save money. Findings indicate that for every instance of low birth weight averted by prenatal care, the United States health-care system saves between $14,000 and $30,000 in health-care system costs associated with this condition.

Nutrition is just as critical as prenatal care in any strong, prevention-oriented health-care approach. Gibbs (1990, p. 47) shares the following insights on the cost of poor nutrition for families and the society.

"Of all the dumb ways of saving money, not feeding pregnant women and kids is the dumbest," says Jean Mayer, one of the world's leading experts on nutrition.During the first year of life, a baby's brain grows to two-thirds its final size. If a baby is denied good, healthy food during this critical period, he or she will need intensive nutritional and developmental therapies to repair the damage.

"A power breakfast for two businessmen is one woman's WIC package for a month," Mayer says. "Why can't public-policy makers see the connection between bad infant nutrition, which is cheap and easy to fix, and developmental problems, which are expensive and often difficult to fix?"

Indeed, the leading debilitating factors in the lives of children (injuries, homicides, learning disabilities) are easier to prevent than to treat. "Poor health" has been cited by two-thirds of teachers as a primary cause of learning problems in young children. In poor populations, teachers cite health, abuse, and drug abuse as factors strongly impeding children's school performance (Gibbs 1990).

The major health problems that parents and young children experience could be mostly precluded through adequate prenatal care, continuing child and family health care, and stronger health education for parents.

## Child Abuse/Neglect

Violence in the home is devastating many children. According to Gibbs (1990, p. 46):

Reports of child abuse have soared from 600,000 in 1979 to 2.4 million in 1989, a searing testimony to the enduring role of children as the easiest victims.

Violence has unfortunately become a part of our cultural system. It is prevalent in many forms: in high use of guns, violent television programming, continued use of physical power to solve problems, highly punitive child discipline, and distorted

103

human relationship ideas (Swick 1987). The drug-abuse epidemic in society has simply added greatly to this problem of violence, and children are the big losers. Vincent Fontana (1992, p. 28) states it clearly:

> Acceptance of public violence has much to do with it. Drug use, of course, has introduced horrendous ramifications. Drugs and alcohol have been a factor in crimes against children for a very long time. But since the early 1980s, substance abuse looms as an increasingly important element in child-abuse cases. More than two-thirds of the states responding to a national survey report drug abuse as a dominant factor in abusing families.

Every type of abuse (physical, sexual, emotional, verbal) presents complex barriers to children, parents, and society as a whole. Abused children perform less effectively in school, have continuing problems with self-image and social relationships, and often end up as antisocial citizens. Abusing and/or abused parents also suffer greatly from this national disease; they are lacking in self-image, often impotent with regard to their emotional development, and in many cases immoral in their family and community actions (Fontana 1992).

The intergenerational nature of abuse and neglect require that early childhood professionals and all citizens attack this barrier with urgent zeal. Leadership and courage are essential to promoting environments where people empower each other rather than abuse each other. As Gibbs (1990, p. 48) says:

> But there will be no real progress, no genuine hope for America's children until the sense of urgency forces a reconsideration of values in every home, up to and including the White House. Polls suggest the will is there: 60 percent of Americans believe the situation for children has worsened over the past five years; 67 percent say they would be more likely to vote for a candidate who supported increased spending for children's programs even if it meant a tax increase.

Abused parents need support programs—particularly counseling, family services, and education. Abused children need caring parents who are competent in social skills. They also need early childhood educators who are nurturing and supportive of total family wellness.

## Preventable Barriers

Poverty, poor health care, low-quality early childhood care, drug abuse, illiteracy, child abuse, and other traditional social and economic barriers are "people-made" constraints. These are not static influences that are beyond our control. We can prevent AIDS through proactive educational practices and sound health/sex practices. Poverty can be constrained through job training, family supports, and intensive educational interventions. High-quality health care and effective early childhood education can make an empowering difference in the lives of parents and children. More prevention efforts in mental health, education, and community enrichment can foster healthier families during the early years.

## SOCIOCULTURAL RISKS AND OPPORTUNITIES

Sociocultural risk means that a person is seriously impeded with regard to the basic social and psychological necessities for functioning in healthy ways (Garbarino 1982). Factors such as poverty, malnutrition, poor health care, and others (as discussed earlier in this chapter) are indicative of this risk. These risks often impede the healthy development of parent-child relationships. Healthy parent-child interactions are typified by reciprocity. This mutuality of caring between parent and child is how we learn acceptable social and cultural values. When this system of mutual, reciprocal caring declines significantly, the balance of "helping relationships" within the family deteriorates (Kerr and Bowen 1988). In a defensive, panic-filled manner, parents tend to "overcontrol" the family when they sense chaos. They often revert to abusive, punitive means of relating to children and to other adults in the family. In effect, the social and cultural fabric of the family is at risk. Parental behavior may be based on past abuse syndromes, lack of needed resources, weak cultural identity, or combinations of these risk factors (Fontana 1992).

Early childhood education has historically provided three resources that have positively influenced the social and cultural orientation of families in productive ways: knowledge, family support and services, and positive role modeling of appropriate ways to relate to children (Dimidjian 1989). Consider, for example, parent-infant relationships. A parent who lacks social and cultural skills for relating to an infant in nurturing ways may become abusive under stress (for lack of knowledge, lack of resources, or both). It might appear in a struggle over feeding or over a diapering experience. Not knowing how to respond, the parent may physically constrain the infant, even become abusive—or totally withdraw and neglect the baby (Fraiberg 1987). With involvement in parenting programs, contacts with trained early childhood or other helping professionals, and through friendly interactions with other nurturing parents, the parent can and often does create more positive ways of handling the normal stressors of infant development (Galinsky 1987).

Sociocultural risk is not rooted in cultural differences but in a lack of a social and cultural history that is inclusive of nurturing and guiding values (Rohner 1986). In this sense, sociocultural risk is present in every segment of our society because of the tremendous history of violence in our culture. Social and cultural mores change gradually, as the history of early childhood education indicates. Provisions for knowledge, supports and services, and positive role modeling are the best tools available for use in tackling this barrier.

Swick (1987) notes that cultural differences in how families nurture and guide their development is usually inclusive of humane and proactive goals and roles. In effect, sociocultural opportunity for family health is desirable in most all cultures. It is typically built into the values and rituals of cultures, at least in an idealistic-directive sense if not in the realities of the daily lives of people. Even in nondemocratic societies, protective and nurturing roles are projected as essential to the intergenerational survival of the culture. In the more "modern" cultures, empowerment of children and families is often projected as essential to the continued creativity and growth of the society.

In the proactive sense, families are envisioned as the foundation of culture, providing the needed continuity of life through nurturance, education, and moral guidance (Blazer 1989). Yet, most cultures allow for diversity of parenting and family functioning in how these goals are achieved. It is also accepted within most societies that families must be supported in carrying out these goals. It is only when cultures lose their value system and/or their essential family-support resources that the healthy functioning of families is threatened. Indeed, the current high levels of family stress are the result of a mixture of the loss of these two forces within our society.

Fontana (1992, pp. 124, 125) describes the decline of these and other forces as they have interacted with the fabric of family life:

> No matter the conformation of the family, the social environment we have created for ourselves in the last two or three decades does not encourage wholesome, stable family life; rather, it tends to poison it.
>
> All the ruptures and frictions that come with a fast-paced and complex society conspire to wear people down. Even people consciously determined to be "good parents" find it extremely difficult to cope with life as it is and their own personal problems, never mind giving the children all the loving care and attention they need.

In spite of the sociocultural barriers that families face in our society, many parents continue against great odds to model and guide children toward being moral and caring persons (Blazer 1989).

## FAMILY DYNAMICS AS A BARRIER

Families, as a result of being a social group, are a social system. As Dunst, Trivette, and Deal (1988) note, most families function on a continuum of strengths and weaknesses. They each develop unique ways of relating to life's stressors, creating a "functioning style" that is responsive to its needs and able to relate to needs in the community. In this framework, there is no right or wrong way of functioning but rather diverse styles of functioning. Along this continuum of family functioning, one can conceptualize that at the extremes there is a theoretical "fully functioning family" and a "dysfunctional family." Most families fall somewhere in between these extremes, being more functional as their style of relationships is in harmony and less functional when it is disruptive (Schwartzman 1985).

Family dynamics become a barrier when they prohibit the actualization of human development of the individuals and the group (Pittman 1987). Every family faces change within the human development system; it is based on growth and change. Most families, however, handle the process of change by accommodating and assimilating events and experiences in some viable manner, albeit unique to their style of living. Given the dramatic rise in stress that families experience, this viability often becomes short-circuited by various factors. These include lack of support, internal pathologies, poor communication, rigid role schemes, and other inhibiting forces (Pittman 1987). When these forces become prevailing rituals within families, the feedback system is distorted and the natural growth processes begin to disintegrate. In a very real sense, when the family feedback system is seriously impeded the family becomes a barrier to itself. What is even more disturbing is that the pattern of family dysfunction initiated when family resources are unable to respond to particular stress can become the basis for long-term pathologies (Swick 1987).

Thus, family dynamics need to be promoted in ways that nurture existing strengths, resolve emerging weaknesses, and foster relationship patterns that promote the family's emotional and spiritual strength (Fowler 1989). Using an empowerment perspective, early childhood educators approach families not from a judgmental position but from a helping and supporting position. The following implications emerge from this approach.

- a focus on family strengths and needs fosters the recognition that all families have resources to use in empowering themselves when they are supported
- a recognition that when family strengths are high-lighted, we as professionals are tapping into the very essence of the "goodness" of that family
- a realization that families get stronger when we are able to capitalize on their strengths
- a recognition that families do respond effectively when they have needed resources and support

The "balance of power" in family dynamics appears to rely on five family elements: communication, emotional commitment, role flexibility, power sharing, and sensitivity to the family's changing developmental continuum (Bradshaw 1988). When these elements become negative forces in the family, family members (as both individual members and as a group) become barriers to each other's healthy growth. The following are examples of family attributes that usually function as barriers to the family's wellness.

- lack of communication or negative communication patterns within family relationships, particularly when this process is persistent
- lack of attachment and emotionally enriching relation-ships within the family structure, particularly when relationships are devoid of caring and are predomi-

109

nantly characterized as abusive

- lack of role exchanges that promote mutuality of internal family support, particularly where roles are rigidly defined in distorted ways
- lack of power sharing within the family's decision-making system, especially where power is located in one person
- lack of adaptation to developmental changes in family members and to the consequent changes in the family's dynamics.

Swick (1991b, p. 113) targets particular relationship patterns that consistently lead to family dysfunction. Evident in Swick's points about dysfunction is the fact that when family dynamics tilt toward negative relationships (always focusing on the deficits in each other), the balance of family well-being is seriously harmed.

> Unhealthy family-relationship systems (which often lead to dysfunctionality) are characterized by their rigidity, insensitivity, and role distortion. Abnormal levels of emotionality along with excessive concentrations of power in one or two family members creates a volatile system, one in which the change process is resisted and often denied. In contrast to the balance of power found in functional families, an extreme imbalance of power is often present in the dysfunctional system. Too much is expected of one or two persons and usually these expectations are based on inappropriate role assignments. In effect, dysfunctional families create excessive stress within their system of relationships by the way they rigidify roles and distort the balance of power. The system is out of balance before external change is ever engaged.

In part, the family's dynamics for relating to change are influenced by external support and resources. A hallmark of dysfunction lies in the family's isolation from external support and resources (Garbarino 1982). Keep in mind that such isolation is intergenerational in that it may have served to protect the family from outside interference, thus isolation becomes associated with survival. When family members do not emotionally connect to those outside the family, they can pretend that they are totally independent from the realities of daily stress. However, this pattern of living ultimately destroys the family because every person and every social system requires nurturance from within and from without (Schwartzman 1985).

A major empowerment force in helping families avoid or resolve intrafamily barriers is that of social support. In particular, emotional, physical, informational, and instrumental support are critical to the family's continued healthy functioning (Cohen and Syme 1985). Sources of support include the many contacts families have or might have in their communities. What is critical is that parents and children see support as healthy and important in their development, both from the needs aspect of it as well as from how they can contribute to the lives of others (Bronfenbrenner 1986).

Relational support, for example, occurs within the family's interactions in the home as well as in members' involvement in work, school, and other situations that might foster relationship strengthening. Consider, for example, the power a teacher has when he or she develops a friendly pattern of relating to a child and the parents of that child. Not only is the teacher creating better family-school relationships but he or she is fostering within family members a healthy perspective about each other (Powell 1989). Of course, the reverse is also true; continued negative teacher-child-parent dynamics can destroy evolving support systems.

There are other types of support that families need. These include structural, constitutional, functional, and support satisfaction (Hall and Wellman 1985). In effect, families need validation, opportunities to develop caring relationships with people beyond the family, and positive experiences with supportive people in their communities. When "family helpers" miss this critical insight (that they need to interrelate with families in supportive ways as perceived by the parents and children), they, too, can become barriers to the family empowerment process (Dunst, Trivette, and Deal 1988).

## FAMILY HELPERS AS BARRIERS

In far too many cases, at-risk families have had the wrong type of help, a type that reinforced their isolation from essential outside resources. Why is this the case when professionals in helping roles attest to be supportive of family wellness? The answer is interrelated with three basic processes: the perceptions of the helpee on what is needed (which are often ignored by the helper), the perceptions of the helper on what is needed (which are often very incomplete and based mostly on limited knowledge), and the dynamics of the helper-helpee relationship (which are often based on an unequal relationship system).

When the family helper is not meeting needs that are seen as important by the family, the helping process can easily become a barrier. Dunst, Trivette, and Deal (1988, p. 8) state:

Responsive and truly individualized interventions address the needs and aspirations of the family by promoting the family's ability to identify and meet its needs in a way that makes the family more capable and competent.

This is especially true in cases of families with "multiple problems." Parents and children typically recognize "needs" within their setting (although they may hide them if they feel overwhelmed). The role of the helper, particularly the professional helper, is to assist families in articulating their concerns and organizing their environment to resolve these stressors (Dunst and Leet 1987).

Incorrect or incomplete perceptions of the helper can distort and impede the family. For example, the teacher may see Rene's problems related to the parent's situation of being a single parent when in reality the parent and child have a good relationship. The problems may be more related to the family's economic situation, which resulted from the father abandoning the family. It is critical that early childhood educators acquire a complete understanding of the family's situation, inclusive of family members' strengths and talents. If the helper sees only the negative aspects of the family, or relies on stereotypes, his or her basis for action is distorted and likely to lead to conflict (Spacapan and Oskamp 1992). Seeking out information through cooperative discussion, respecting family requests for privacy, sharing possible resources for family strengthening, and taking into account the "family perspective" are proactive approaches.

> Help givers are expected to be positive, see the strengths of help seekers, and assist help seekers to see their potential and capabilities. This is all done in a cooperative, partnership approach that emphasizes joint responsibility between the help seeker and the help giver (Dunst, Trivette, and Deal 1988, p. 44).

Above all, a lack of caring is certain to dull any helping relationship. Parents and children "doubt" the validity and credibility of helpers who distort, dominate, and/or degrade their family. Gossip, jumping to conclusions, and putting the family on the defensive usually indicate the helper does not have an accurate view of the family's needs and strengths.

Finally, helper-helpee relationships that are unequal (dominated by the helper) foster negative and debilitating partnerships. Attitude and a "sense of mutuality" are everything in the helping process (Fisher, Nedler, and Whitcher-Alagna 1983). Early childhood educators actually impede the family when they treat them with disdain or even subtle disrespect. It is vital that we know the cultural values, family interests, and sensitive issues of concern to parents and child when attempting to be a part of their lives (Caldwell 1989). Communication needs to foster an equal relationship system, one that encourages sharing, cooperation, and support for each other. Swick (1991b, pp. 144–45) describes the essence of early childhood educators' task in this partnership process:

> The essential element in successful partnerships with at-risk families is the communication process. Far too often teachers use a directed, authority-based form of communicating with parents. While such a form of communication is ineffective with parents in general, it is disastrous with at-risk parents. Highly formal, authoritative communication too often lacks the two major components vital to involving at-risk parents in meaningful partnerships: closeness and mutuality. Parents under heavy stress need the closeness that exists in responsive, supportive, and sensitive communication. They also need a feeling of mutuality, a sense of togetherness with significant others as they attempt to resolve problems and stressors.

## Models Used in Helping

Brickman and his colleagues (1982, 1983; Karuza, Zevon, Rabinowitz, and Brickman 1982; Rabinowitz, Karuza, and Zevon 1984) provide a description of the four "models" used in helping relations. Early childhood educators need to examine these modes of helping so they can avoid becoming a barrier in this process. The four models are: moral, medical, enlightenment, and compensatory. The distinguishing features of each model relate to how the help seeker is held responsible for causing problems and whether or not the help seeker is held responsible for solving the problems.

In the *moral model*, help seekers are held responsible for creating as well as solving problems. This perspective places the total responsibility on the help seeker, the help giver sees his or her role as moralizing. While this approach might empower, it is more likely to cause parents to feel as though the burden is on them without any support. Isolation and burnout are likely outcomes of this model's thinking.

114

In the *medical model,* help seekers are neither responsible for problems nor for solutions. Believers in this model feel that physical and psychological problems are illnesses, diseases, or aberrations that only trained experts can understand, diagnose, and treat. In this perspective, the help seeker is likely to attribute positive changes to the help giver. Dependence, passivity, and feelings of helplessness are possible negative outcomes of this approach.

The *enlightenment model* promotes the idea that help seekers are responsible for their problems and are capable of solving them with the help and support of others. This approach requires others to remind the help seeker of their mistakes and to assist them in the maintenance and corrective action process. Likely consequences of this model include lowered self-esteem and a sense of incompetence or guilt.

Help seekers are viewed as innocent victims who are not responsible for their problems, but are responsible for their solutions in the *compensatory model.* Programs such as Head Start and CETA (Comprehensive Educational Training Association) are based on this model. It emphasizes the help seekers acquisition of self-sustaining behaviors and self-efficacy. Potential outcomes include increased self-esteem and enhanced social competence.

Clearly, the different models connote different ways of relating to families in at-risk situations. Obviously, some models promote barriers to empowerment while others foster a strengthening process. The ecological-empathetic approach advocated in this book emphasizes collective influences as "cause" and a partnership approach as "solution." The focus is on supporting help seekers in articulating their needs and then in creating necessary self-other systems to empower themselves. The dignity and autonomy of the individual and the family are respected through a shared-learning process. In effect, we are about the process of strengthening each other through mutually responsive relationships (Swick 1991b).

115

# THE SEEDS OF HEALTHY FAMILIES

Every family has the potential to be healthy. Even in the midst of the stress experienced by families, there are signs of health. Perhaps the weight of the barriers experienced mask these traits of wellness, or possibly as professionals we fail to look for the seeds of health that truly exist. Insights into the healthy attributes of at-risk families who are able to resolve risks and overcome even major barriers are instructive of the directions early childhood professionals should pursue in their educational and support efforts. Research has identified some key elements of "healthy family behaviors" that are pervasive among at-risk families who rise above the pressures of the risk situations they confront.

In particular, an emotional and social attachment among family members is present in healthy families (Caldwell 1989, Honig 1989). This is especially evident in at-risk families who consistently overcome the many barriers of poverty and other stress factors (Benard 1992, Werner 1987). Bonding and attachment behaviors of the mother appear to be the critical beginning point of healthy family life; they appear to buffer the family from the harsh realities of the environment. This process is multidirectional in that children and parents benefit from it and it is a lifelong factor when nurtured in a continuing way. Werner (1987, p. 40) says:

> We were impressed by the pervasive effects of the quality of the mother-child interaction in infancy and early childhood that were documented as early as year one by home visitors and that were verified independently by the psychologists during the developmental examinations in the second year. They were also noted by the classroom teachers at age 10, and commented on by the youth in the age 18 interview.

Father attachment is also critical, although it may initially show up in the form of high support for the mother and in joyful

116

play times with the infant. Perhaps the strongest attribute of resilient families in at-risk situations is this emotional, social, and spiritual commitment to each other (Fowler 1989).

Competent parenting or the presence of another capable, caring adult is another key attribute of at-risk families who exhibit resilience in the face of serious problems (Garmezy 1992). The value of a capable, mature, and involved parent is very powerful in any family, particularly in cases where the family is facing tremendous chronic stress. Burton White (1988) notes that parents play the key roles in establishing the healthy personality in young children. He points to parental involvement in meeting basic nurturance, health, and physical needs; nurturing the child in loving and caring ways; stimulating the child through appropriate learning experiences; and guiding and monitoring the child's behavior and development. Swick (1987 1991b) suggests that parental competence in at-risk families makes the difference because this sets the tone for a positive and optimistic approach to life. It is not an issue of biological parenthood but rather an issue of having a caring, capable adult in the "parenting role" who is, as Bronfenbrenner (1979) says "irrationally in love with the child." Benard (1992, p. 6) sums it up well:

> What is evident is that to mitigate the effects of other risks and stressful life events and to develop healthily, a child needs the "enduring loving involvement of one or more adults in care and joint activity with that child."

Not surprisingly, healthy families (even within at-risk environments) have meaningful and effective social supports with friends, relatives, or some source in the community (Pence 1988). In particular, parents (or whomever is performing the parenting role) establish the validity of using the environment as a source of problem solving. It is a type of modeling that influences everyone in the family positively. Curran (1985, p. 48) provides some valuable insight in this regard:

117

Clearly, the most stress-effective families make the most use of support systems. When they need sudden child care, or when there's an illness or a problem, they have people to call upon, people who will call upon them as freely in turn.

The influence of extra-family supports is evident in everyone's functioning. Parents function more effectively because they have access to significant people they trust. Children perform better also, mainly because they sense a connecting relationship to the world beyond the family. This support network is most critical when serious problems exist within the family. In some cases it is an alternate care giver (a grandparent or another relative) who provides the child with a buffer from the harsh problems of life (Werner 1987).

Healthy families "expect the best" from each other, that is, they anticipate and communicate high expectations to each other (Swick 1987). This is particularly the case with parental expectations of children. Benard (1992, p. 6) points out:

Research into why some children growing up in poverty still manage to be successful in school and in young adulthood has consistently identified high parental expectations as the contributing factor.

In healthy families, parents expect moral behavior from their children and act accordingly. These families have a continuing spiritual and moral life, a set of rituals that nurture their faith and promote a hopeful view of life. It very importantly gives children the security of knowing that the adults around them care enough to set the pace for living a moral life. It should not be surprising then that high-achieving poor children live in families who have high expectations and match those expectations with support and guidance (Lickona 1992).

In effect, healthy families work at developing strong relationships. They develop and use the following relationship elements throughout their lives: trust, role flexibility, help-exchange behaviors, responsive listening, encouragement of individual achievement, group-functioning skills, nurturance of each other, and shared problem solving (Swick 1991b). In this same regard, healthy families integrate the following characteristics into their lives.

- love
- religiosity
- respect
- communication
- individuality
- togetherness
- consideration
- commitment
- sharing
- parental competence

Most critically, healthy families promote the importance of positive self-esteem in each other. They actively help each other develop a positive self-concept.

## NEW PERSPECTIVES ON REMOVING BARRIERS

All children and all families confront barriers to their full and healthy development. It is the intensity, quantity, timing, and manner in which they experience these barriers that can create an at-risk and eventually "high-risk" situation (Curran 1985, Garmezy and Rutter 1983, Hamburg 1992). Twenty years of research that has tracked the development of at-risk syndromes points to the fact that barriers have their most dramatic impact on children and families during the family's formative period. It is during this period that barriers bring their full power to erode family and individual development, particularly when family resources are inadequate to the tasks at hand. It is also apparent that "barriers," once engrained in family-living patterns, become entangled with other barriers and create a mosaic of elements that promulgates risks and eventually, dysfunction (Magid and

119

McKelvey 1988). Alcoholism, for example, typically creates a relationship system that advances violence and abuse. Poor nutrition during pregnancy increases the likelihood of low birth weight, which in turn reduces the infant's viability, thus increasing the potential for many other problems (Thompson and Hupp 1992).

Research has also noted that particular developmental and ecological events seem to foster less resiliency to the power of barriers (Ford and Lerner 1992, Hamburg 1992). For example, a "teen parent" is generally more vulnerable to the stresses of economic and social change than a more mature and experienced parent. Economically poor parents are more vulnerable to other stressors, typically because poverty breeds higher crime, less social opportunity, and more family risks (Thompson and Hupp 1992). In the same perspective, it is now understood that "barriers" can become intergenerational life-styles, especially when these patterns of living become accepted as beliefs and values. Thus, removing barriers to the empowerment of families is a holistic process and must be the business of every citizen.

Emerging from this better understanding of how barriers to healthy family and child development take hold are some perspectives on how they can best be manipulated, resolved, and possibly prevented. What follows are brief descriptions of some of the most useful perspectives on the removal of barriers to the family's development. They represent "achievable" perspectives through the sensitive action of every community.

## Parent Education for All

The most insidious barrier to child and family wellness is parental incompetence (Magid and McKelvey 1988, Spivack and Cianci 1987). In the broader sense, this process can be expanded to include adult incompetence as related to the nurturance of children (Albee 1992). That's because every adult is to some degree a "parent" in that all adults are members of the community. It is in this way of thinking that a "parent education for all" notion is presented. Most barriers that restrict child and family development are open to manipulation and intervention by parents and other adults. Benard (1992) points to effective parenting as the key to the prevention of multiple other risk factors. It is parents and other caring adults who prevent or rectify the barriers that count the most during the early childhood years. Through the application of White's (1988) basic principles of parenting, families do become empowered. All types of families from different social, economic, and cultural contexts nurture very young children and themselves toward a moral and productive life.

A parent education for all perspective calls for early and continuing education for parents and a continual "child and family wellness" theme within the community. The basic emphases are to provide children with basic health and nutrition, nurture and love them continuously, interact with them in mutual and respectful ways, promulgate family caring rituals, involve children in enriching learning experiences, and provide them with the best moral guidance possible (White 1988). Likewise, every citizen in the community needs to be educated for a value orientation that says: "We must support children and families in a way that assures them of a full and healthy life" (Albee 1992). Parents can only carry out their empowerment mission when the other adults around them are fully supportive. This orientation means that in every community adults who are close to families are involved with them in the raising of children in positive ways. It also means that programs have other adults in the world of business engaged in interacting regularly with children as tutors, friends, and helpers (Swick 1991b).

## An Empowerment Foundation in Every Community

Based on what we now know about preventing barriers at the start of life (Thompson and Hupp 1992) and on the current negative impact particular barriers are having on young parents and their children (The Annie E. Casey Foundation 1992), we can and must create an empowerment foundation for healthy family life in every community. Removing the presence of potential barriers before they become a reality is the best strategy for any society. Thompson and Hupp provide a four-dimensional framework that offers an empowerment foundation: remove environmental hazards (e.g., lead poisoning), reduce adolescent pregnancy and childbirth, provide high quality prenatal care, and reduce the incidence of low birth weight. The following are actions that need to be carried out within these areas (Thompson and Hupp 1992, Chapter 10).

### Table 3.1:
### Empowerment Action Areas That Provide
### A Strong Family Foundation

**Environmental Hazards**
- Ban all alcoholic beverage advertising.
- Conduct antismoking campaigns.
- Maintain constant antismoking campaign with at-risk populations.
- Control environmental toxins (for example, lead removal).
- Provide drug prevention and AIDS education and services.

**Adolescent Pregnancy/Childbirth**
- Provide communitywide sex and family education.
- Offer adolescent counseling and support on sex and family life.
- Practice high self-esteem education for all, but especially for at risk.
- Set up family-planning clinics in all at-risk neighborhoods.

**Prenatal Care**
- Make prenatal care available to all through Medicaid.
- Provide communitywide prenatal care education.
- Set up community prenatal care-centers in all high-risk neighborhoods.
- Organize interagency case management of populations prone to poor prenatal care.

## Low Birth Weight
- Advocate keeping adolescents in school.
- Use WIC and other programs to support proper nutrition during pregnancy.
- Make prenatal care available to all who are at risk.
- Coordinate community action to prevent low birth weight.

## *Empowerment from Within: Resources in At-Risk Settings*

Research on the "helping process" clearly indicates that the most effective and lasting changes in families and schools occur when the process is controlled and guided from within the system itself (Spacapan and Oskamp 1992). Typically, at-risk families are indeed powerful within their own system. Often, the problem is organizing their resources and environment to become powerful in their transactions with the broader society. In fact, those at risk often have more problem-solving skills than nonrisk populations; they simply have not found ways to mobilize their skills and resources for use in interacting with other systems (Swick 1987, 1991b).

We need to feel wanted and important in order to be able to help others and ourselves. It is this maxim that offers a key insight on how many barriers can be removed, and at the same time, promotes a new sense of power in families. Putting parents, children, and young people in positions of helping others actually stimulates in them new skills (or renewed skills) for use in solving their own problems. This is particularly effective when such activities are guided by people they see as successful and as a part of their life. Mentor programs, foster-grandparent projects, adopt-a-teen parent projects, big brothers/big sisters, youth as resources, parent networking, guided self-help, and neighborhood helper programs all exemplify this concept. Calhoun (1992, p. 338) describes some of the positive outcomes of a Youth as Resources (YAR) project:

123

YAR youth confront social issues by presenting plays about drug-abuse prevention, organizing outings for children living in shelters for battered women, helping in construction of quality low-income housing, providing services for shut-ins, serving as "buddies" for children in foster care, taking on community beautification projects, and growing vegetables for a food bank. Youth are partnered with adults to tackle every social issue in the community.

There are other encouraging happenings, such as former drug addicts mentoring teen parents in a drug prevention program, an abused mother coordinating a spouse abuse networking project, and a classroom teacher returning to "her neighborhood" to tutor and befriend children at risk for school failure.

Comer and Haynes (1991) provide numerous examples of how "involved parents" can take ownership in the education of their children through greater participation in the governance of schools, through active involvement in classroom roles (including some teaching roles), and through positive and responsive relationships with teachers. Fraiberg (1987) achieved similar empowerment goals with abusing mothers by involving them in designing their own individual goals. She found that as they learned to use their "inner resources," they not only became more nurturing with their babies but more responsive to their own needs, too!

## Self-Concept and Social Competence as Curriculum

School and society often get lost in "outcome measures" that typically mask more serious human development issues. Thus, our fetish with the low test scores of at-risk children or our erroneous judgment of mothers on welfare. Yet, every major study on successful at-risk children or on the effective removal of barriers to school and life failure mark two critical process areas: self-esteem and social competence (Benard 1992). Becoming a positive and caring person requires early childhood experiences that establish these directions as desirable and achievable. And this process begins at birth. Without positive self-esteem, families are in trouble from the outset. Following are self-esteem building strategies that can be pursued in every community.

- Promote parent-child attachment through pre-birth parenting programs in multiple ways: through courses for parents, public announcements, newspaper reminders, school literature, and most critically, by modeling healthy emotional and moral behavior for others.

- Make the self-esteem of children in early childhood programs the top priority of the curriculum, of staff concerns, and of the total school-family effort. Use every opportunity possible to foster in children a feeling of self-importance and positive mental health.

- Encourage business and community groups to place the self-esteem of their workers and helpers at the top of their priority list. Reward parents for being positive and involved in children's lives. Encourage citizens to be positive examples for each other.

- Sponsor and foster "positive self-esteem rituals" in family, school, and community. Children's fairs, positive parenting awards, citizen-recognition days, and other such practices can offer models for living in empowering ways.

Social competence evolves from people who think highly of themselves and others. It, too, begins in the cradle and must be nurtured within the total ecology of human development. Parents are the primary source of children's guidance toward social competence during the early childhood years. Swick and Duff (1982, p. 6) describe the central roles of parents.

Any effort directed toward helping children become nurturing in their behavior must begin in infancy. Infants learn to trust and feel secure by the way they are treated by those adults significant to them. Parents who provide warm nurturing care

125

to their infant are establishing a human bond vital to the child's later formation of attitudes, values, and behavior.

Social competence includes two basic processes: respect and responsibility. These two processes require empathy, a sensitivity to the needs of others, the ability to guide one's own behavior in positive ways, and a responsiveness to the needs of the total community. For children to acquire these basic behaviors, they need to be around adults who expect and model such behaviors. These are developmental processes that call for a supportive experience with others. Lickona (1992, p. 73) gives the example of Bill Rose, a teacher who through modeling a caring and supportive approach is able to reach at-risk children and families.

> Bill Rose's classroom is testimony to the power of treating students with love and respect. His students talk of how the class is "a family," how they don't come late, how they have straightened themselves out and gotten their grades up, and how they work hard for Mr. Rose because he cares about them and they don't want to let him down. They are learning about the meaning of respect and love by experiencing them firsthand.

Everyone must value children and families as the developers of social competence. It must become a priority of our daily lives, not just something we expect to happen periodically.

## "Community as Family": Breaking Down Barriers

We need to be aggressive in our communities in promoting moral living through nurturing and enriching environments. Our families have changed, our workplaces have changed, and now it is time to change how we support children and families. In the past we have invested tremendous energy in building massive military defense-systems. We did so with tremendous ingenuity. We can and must put this energy and creativity to work on building communities where human dignity is our very first concern. Families and communities, as Popenoe (1988, pp. 337-338) notes, are reciprocal systems that "feed each other" in both the positive and negative sense. Without strong communities, families face troubled times, and the reverse is true as well.

> Because of the reciprocal relationships among these mediating structures, it is no wonder that as one withers, so do the others. Strong neighborhoods, churches, and voluntary associations are a rarity without the presence of strong families; they weaken as families in an area weaken. By the same token, the family can be weakened as these larger structures decline.

Prevention and the resolution of barriers that are precluding at-risk families from healthy living are only feasible through their participation in total community action. Schools and communities must transform how they relate to at-risk populations and more control and responsibility must be engendered in families and children. This can only occur as communities and schools expect and then foster this full participation design. Stark (1992, p. 173) tells of the experience of one such approach (Munich's Healthy Cities Project):

> We started a series of laboratories with children, youth, and adults to develop perspectives on the city from the grass-roots level. These Future Labs are both planning instruments and tools for envisioning, an attempt to stimulate the social fantasy of citizens in order to encourage them to create and shape their own (physical and social) environment.

He goes on to describe a conference planned and run by children and youth (p. 173):

> The conference program included talk shows, excursions to

127

industrial plants, various workshops, and radio and television programs, culminating in the city's first Kids' Forum in Munich's City Hall—all performed by children and youth. They took the leading part during the conference (adults have been admitted only as resource persons), discussing their issues with politicians and city officials.

Many other examples exist of community and school initiatives that reach out for this full participation ethic. Head Start is perhaps one of the best examples of a program that attempts to gain its mission through parent-citizen leadership (Powell 1989). Edwards and Young (1992) offer some excellent reaching out examples (1992, pp. 78-79).

In Donaldsonville, the missing link was forged by a program created by a local university professor who never accepted the assumption of parents' lack of interest in their children's success. She solicited community support to attract parents to a reading program, where they would be assisted in learning how to read and how to read with their children.

She called on community leaders to recruit parents they knew in contexts outside the school. Church leaders black and white, agreed to preach from their pulpits about the importance of helping children learn to read.

A local bar owner emerged as a strong supporter of the reading program, informing mothers who patronized his establishment that they would no longer be welcome unless they put as much time into learning how to read to their children as they spent enjoying themselves at his bar. He provided transportation to school and back home for participating mothers and secured funds from the city for parents who otherwise could not attend. A grandmother organized a campaign to telephone program participants each week. In sum, the bridge that connected home and school was found in the broader community.

The barriers that prevent healthy child and family

development are resolvable when total community involvement is directed toward this end. Drug havens can be replaced with youth centers; AIDS is preventable through education about safe sexual practices; family violence can be transformed into harmony through social values and supports that promote moral and nurturing ways of living; poverty can be reduced through adult literacy, job training, and related strategies; and many other problems can be solved when citizens act in concert to make healthy communities a priority.

# Chapter 4

# INSIGHTS ON RELATING TO THE NEEDS OF AT-RISK FAMILIES

Each family in an at-risk situation has its own style of functioning regardless of its similarity to others. Certainly the "risks" and "barriers" explored thus far in this book present the types of stressors and challenges faced by at-risk families. And the types of prevention and empowerment ideas offered represent effective ways of relating to children and families. Beyond these perspectives, however, are the intricate aspects of the way each family lives, how the family responds to its particular situation, and how it and its helpers attempt to resolve or prevent risks. Much can and has been learned from studying individual families who are in at-risk situations. The primary function of this chapter is to explore the individual family situations of at-risk parents and children, and to share particular insights on how early childhood professionals attempted to engage in empowering relationships with them.

Included in this discussion are case-study examples of at-risk families as observed and studied by the authors. Integrated into the examples are pertinent insights that have been synthesized from the literature on at-risk families. The case presentations are shared with the realization that no single response to family stress is adequate. Rather, they are presented with the idea that others might benefit from studying them and from their own critical analysis of how they might improve on the strategies and insights applied to these cases. The following are basic premises that the material presented attempts to articulate.

- Each family is unique! While there are common patterns of functioning in at-risk families, the unique conditions and functioning style of each family needs to be known if early childhood educators are to be effective (Kerr and Bowen 1988).

- At-risk families typically have strengths that are overshadowed by their apparent problems. Early childhood professionals need to look for and capitalize on the family's strengths. Only as parents and children see their own talents and skills valued by others do they gain the confidence to resolve their problems (Dunst, Trivette, and Deal 1988).

- Prevention of at-risk family scenarios is best realized during the family's formative period if and when community supports are strong. Most such scenarios have their origins in the family's first two years of life. Prevention emphases can channel energy toward family empowerment before poor relationship patterns are formed (Garbarino 1982).

- Helping professionals such as early childhood educators need to see the parent-professional relationship as an equal, reciprocal partnership. We learn and gain as much from parents and children as they gain from us. Helping relationships should be based on trust, respect, and mutual concerns (Swick 1991b).

- The helping process is based on trust and mutual respect for each person's dignity. Empowerment requires human partnerships where people value and support each other in ways that promote growth and harmony. This calls for sensitive problem solving where everyone is involved in articulating problems and solutions (Albee 1992).

- Resolving risk situations in families requires time, trust building, resources, active listening, patience, encouragement, and shared problem solving. In effect, working with children and families who are under heavy stress requires planning and time-intensive efforts. This in turn calls for new staffing and structural designs in our various helping professions (Fontana 1992).

- Like any human learning process, working with at-risk families is a systems process where professionals and families must examine and act on the total picture. Every aspect of child and family relationships is interrelated with the others; every child brings his or her family to school (Bronfenbrenner 1979).

- Supporting families in resolving even small risk factors in positive ways leads to a family-strengthening process and positions everyone for further positive involvement. At-risk children and families have a sharp focus on both positive and negative events; they register even the smallest helping situation and use it to further strengthen their system (Galinsky 1988).

- Moving beyond the stereotypes often associated with at-risk families is critical to forming effective relationships and strategies with families. Stereotypes often focus on the negative and foster distrust. Learning about the strengths and needs of families through their perspectives brings with it more faith in each other and the empowerment process (Kagan and Schlosberg 1989).

These premises provide a set of perspectives that are further developed in the following case examples. Each case is presented in two parts: information on the context of the family and insights on how early childhood professionals engaged the family in proactive ways to address their situation.

## POOR AND ISOLATED, BUT CARING AND CONCERNED

This case took place in a rural community in a primary school that had received funding to develop more effective ways of involving at-risk parents in their children's education. One of the strategies involved the use of a trained home visitor who worked with selected families in an in-depth manner on any family issues that might positively influence the children's school success. The home visitor worked with a team of teachers and was an integral part of the educational program. A supportive and proactive family-school partnership was promoted as a part of the school's total curriculum efforts.

## The Context

Mary Rand is a single parent who lives with her mother in a very small, deteriorating house about 10 miles from the school. Her husband left her and the three children after he was fired from a local logging firm —at the time of the birth of the third child. The children are now two, five, and seven years old. Mary is 32 and has not completed high school. She is intelligent and has shown remarkable skills in guiding the family. She is, however, overwhelmed and unable to come to terms with the family's severe economic problems. She is unemployed and has never applied for family assistance. The family is dependent on the grandmother's social security check. There is no heat in the house and an obvious shortage of food. The house is clean and neat. It is very small with two bedrooms and a general living area.

The family goes to church at least weekly. This is their primary social contact outside the home. They live in a very isolated area, and the children have no playmates except each other. They are very shy, obedient, and responsive, but clearly delayed in language and general knowledge skills. They are good listeners and function adequately in the classroom with regard to behavior. However, all three children are at risk academically. The family reads the Bible weekly and is interested in literacy. Family members simply lack the resources to acquire books or the daily newspaper.

The family has strong and positive emotional and spiritual relationships. Members are warm and nurturing and supportive of each other. The mother has worked diligently to help the family overcome the father's abuse and abandonment. All three children are underweight for their age, and they each need medical attention. None of the children nor the mother has had medical care since the birth of the last child. Only the grandmother has medical insurance.

At the school, family members are known as "isolates" who don't cause any problems. The sensitive and caring teacher who referred the family to our family-support project said, "The children and mother need lots of help. They have been through hell and are still very positive. They need attention, but they are not isolates, they are simply afraid!" She also said that this was a family that could really benefit from the family-strengthening project.

## Helping Insights

Prior to the involvement of Mary Rand in the school's Teacher-Parent Partnership Project for parents of children at risk of school failure, she had very few interactions with teachers or other school personnel. The program was structured so that a trained home visitor and the children's teachers (kindergarten and first grade) "team up" to develop a plan for strengthening the family's involvement in the educational process. In the case of the Rand family, the home visitor proved to be the key intervention person. She was a member of the same church as Mary Rand and was familiar with the family's situation. She met Mary at church and invited her to be a part of the school's new program. Mary accepted, but explained she did not have a car and could not get to the school. The home visitor assured her that she would help out with that need.

The early home visits were focused on building a trusting relationship and explaining the program. The home visitor started by praising Mary for the love and guidance she had given the children and by explaining that the focus of the program was on doing everything possible to support the family and help the children have a successful school experience. Mary Rand explained that they were a poor but happy family, especially since the father left. She knew that "social services" was watching them, she said. The home visitor explained that she was there to help and not to interfere with the family's wishes in any way. She also explained that Mary could get involved in several different ways, but could schedule things according to her family's needs. They developed a good relationship and over the first few months of the program developed a very supportive partnership. The home visitor helped the family take care of some very basic needs. She

- had the heat turned on with funds from a community group,
- acquired some good used clothes for Mary and the children through a program at the church,
- assisted the family in signing up for available government-aid programs, (This took some time as Mary had to be convinced that this was not stealing from other people but rather a way of helping her and the children get on their feet.)
- acquired a used car for Mary through help from the church,
- acquired books and magazines for the home through the county's literacy program, and
- nurtured Mary to get involved in the school's partnership program through monthly home visits, in-school activities, home-learning activities, and conferences with the children's teachers.

Eventually, Mary Rand enrolled in a GED program and completed her high school equivalency. She also took a part-time job in the school's cafeteria where she met some new friends. The children received badly needed medical care; made progress in physical, social, and academics; and were happier children by far. Certainly a key to this family's progress was its underlying emotional and spiritual strength. Yet the support and involvement of the home visitor and other school staff (particularly the classroom teachers) as well as church and community members was a significant empowerment influence. Through support and mutual efforts, the family was able to overcome its isolation, attend to some basic needs, actualize some of its literacy interests, and become more effectively involved in the school. Following are helping insights mentioned by the home visitor and the classroom teachers.

- Know and respect the family's situation!
- Work on establishing a trusting relationship with the family.
- Attend to the specific basic needs of the family first!
- Build a partnership with the parent(s).
- Give families time to integrate new behaviors and values.

## ABUSED AND SICK, BUT DETERMINED AND HOPEFUL

This case took place in a small community preschool parent-education program. The program was designed to help "high-risk" parents resolve major risk factors in their lives, in hope of creating the basis for stronger and healthier family relationships. This is a spouse-abuse case that may exist more often than any of us thinks possible. It also represents the underlying intergenerational stream of violence and abuse that permeates our cultural values.

### The Context

Helen Bates is 27 and has two children. She lives with a 55-year-old farmer in an isolated rural area. He owns a small farm that is about 20 miles from town. While he earns a good living, the house is in disrepair, and Helen and the children live in dire poverty. The children were fathered by a previous boyfriend. "The Boss" took her in as his live-in friend. He does not like the children, but lets them stay on the farm. He is abusive, a heavy drinker, and pretty much an isolate. Helen is not allowed to go to town except to get food, which is not very often. A social services worker has visited the home twice in the past year, but has avoided confronting "The Boss."

Helen has been quite sick and is in need of surgery. The children are seriously delayed in all aspects of development and are poorly nourished. They have been totally isolated except for television. They have few social skills. "The Boss" has physically and sexually abused Helen in front of the children and has threatened to kill her should she try to leave.

When the oldest child did not show up for first grade, the teacher talked with the home visitor in the preschool parenting-program and asked her to look into the situation. This simple request provided the impetus for the school's involvement with this family. The home visitor talked with social services, which was aware of the family's situation and offered to help her make contact with the family.

## Helping Insights

A phone call from the home visitor got this response from Helen: "He won't let me bring my boy to school. Can you come talk with him? Can you come to the house?" The home visitor and the child's teacher went together to the home for the first visit. "The Boss" (he was known throughout the area by this name and would not respond to any other name) was gone when they arrived for the visit. They introduced themselves to Helen and the children and gave each child a literacy bag (these were given to each family participating in the program). These bags included crayons, paper, books, pencils, and other materials. They explained that they were part of the school's new program to support families and that their role was to be of help.

Helen explained that "The Boss" was odd—and abusive. But she had nothing else; she had been thrown out by her former boyfriend. She said, "We have to get out of here." But she feared for what would happen to her and the children if they tried to leave. And anyway, where would they go? She also explained that her stomach was giving her real problems; she knew she needed surgery. Helen was distraught, but very loving; the children hung to her in supportive ways. They were indeed partners trying to make the best of a very difficult situation.

The home visitor explained that she could help. She explained to Helen what the program was about and how the program could be helpful to her and the children. Through this initial visit, the home visitor learned that Helen never finished high school, had been sexually abused as a child, was totally isolated on the farm, and that she wanted badly to leave "The Boss," but feared for what might happen to them. Helen, she learned, was a strong person who was in need of urgent help. In spite of all the trauma Helen had been through, she was a loving person who had many skills buried beneath the self-image problems she was experiencing.

Two days after the visit, the home visitor got a call from Helen. "We got to get out of here," she said. "He got mean last night and hurt me badly." The home visitor had talked with social services after the first visit and called again after this call from Helen. Together they went to the home to see what could be done immediately to help the family. Helen had been bruised badly and was in tears. Because the community had no emergency shelter for abused families, the home visitor suggested that she could get a small apartment in town where they could stay until more permanent arrangements could be made. The social worker said he could somehow arrange for emergency aid for food and basic needs. That very day the family moved to town. "The Boss" was never heard from again. He was visited by the local police and warned to never go near Helen and the children or he would be jailed.

The home visitor went to work on helping the family make a new and more stable life. She helped them set up the needed connections to get family aid and the supports needed to function effectively. She also made dinner for them one evening and read to the children. In effect, she became a close partner with the family over the next few months. The most important need she met was that of emotionally nurturing Helen and the children. She talked with the first grader's teacher, and together they mapped out some strategies for helping him build self-confidence. They also put together some enjoyable preschool books for the younger child. Between the two of them, they made a major difference in the life of this family. Very critically, the home visitor helped Helen

- get to a physician to make arrangements for the surgery Helen needed,
- acquire a place in a low-rent housing unit that would be stable for the family,
- organize a family schedule that promoted order and active involvement in the school and community,
- meet new friends at church and school functions,
- attend to the medical needs of the children,
- enroll the youngest child in the school's child-development program, and
- acquire needed clothing and other essential resources.

As the family was able to find some stability in its new setting, the home visitor began to integrate educational activities into the home visits. New books, games, magazines, library resources, and other "in-the-home" activities were used. Tutoring was arranged for the first grader, and the mother was enrolled in an adult-education course. Social services, although very limited in resources, did help in accessing counseling services for the mother and summer-enrichment opportunities for the children.

While the family still faces many problems (of which the healing from past abuse is certainly a priority), members have progressed dramatically over the past year. The oldest child made tremendous progress and is "in-grade" for his age group. Most importantly, he is becoming socially involved and an active learner. He still has difficulty asserting himself, but has grown dramatically in this regard. The mother and younger child also have made gains. With the barrier of abuse lifted, and with the help of a nurturing home visitor, this family's future looks very hopeful. In less than three months, the mother has gained 10 pounds, and both children have gained weight. They have joined a local church and have helped operate the parent nights at school. The home visitor offers the following insights in regard to being an effective family helper.

- Be aware of the "signs of abuse" and report it immediately!
- Provide the family with at least one nurturing, continuing helper!
- Be positive and optimistic in your relationships with the family.
- Help the family connect with the school and community.

## A BITTER FATHER AND A NURTURING STEPMOTHER: OVERCOMING POST-DIVORCE TRAUMA

This case took place in an early childhood laboratory-program operated by a university that is located in a midsize city. It represents only one of the many scenarios that happen in families where divorce and remarriage occur during the child's early years. In particular, it shows what can be accomplished when the problems of families are addressed early in the child's development, and it provides some insights on how schools can work with families on difficult and sensitive issues.

### The Context

Lisa seems to be a typical kindergarten child, running and playing with the other children on the playground. Yet, later in the day she breaks into hysteria—crying (sobbing) and withdrawing to a corner of the classroom. She displays masturbation motions and rejects the comfort her teachers try to offer. She soon settles down and is back to being a member of the class. Initially, Lisa had one episode a day, but soon these tantrumlike periods grew and began to happen two, three, and four times a day. Lisa, as we were to find out later, was caught in the middle of a postdivorce conflict that was related to the two years of family upheaval that led to the divorce. It only took the staff a few days to realize Lisa had some very serious problems.

Through the family-history interview (which the school requires of all participating families) it was learned that the father (Bill) had divorced about a year ago and had remarried about two months prior to Lisa's entrance to school. At the time of the interview, the father was brief in his discussion of the divorce, only saying that it was very hard on him and Lisa. He had retained custody of Lisa, but at that point, did not elaborate. Clearly, the father was not ready or willing to give the teaching staff the total picture at that time. It was obvious that he was very caring toward Lisa and happy in his new marriage.

Bill was a successful sales director, about 32, and well educated. His new wife (Karen) was an executive assistant in a computer firm, very personable, and also well educated. She had just turned 31, and this was her first marriage. Lisa was the only child in Bill's previous marriage, and she was clearly a central focus in his life. The family had no major economic problems, just the normal financial stress that upper-middle-class families experience. The new marriage appeared very strong and was a source of sanity and strength for Bill.

While there were definitely some emotional conflicts present in Bill and Lisa (extending from the divorce and prior family-system influences), there were also some very obvious strengths. It was evident from the start that Bill cared deeply for Lisa and wanted only the best life possible for her. It was equally clear that he and his new wife Karen loved each other and that Lisa was important to both of them. Yet, there were ghosts of the divorce experience still very present in the lives of all three of them. There were strong conflicts in and between the father-child-mother triad of the first marriage/family that were psychologically preventing the emergence of stability and harmony in the new family. Initially, Bill denied these realities, and this prevented the staff from being effective helpers early on in this situation.

Several dysfunctional patterns were present in the first family that were still haunting Bill, Lisa, and indirectly, Karen. The school staff was not aware of these issues until they were later revealed in conferences.

- The mother (Jean) in the first marriage was an alcoholic.
- She had boyfriends over often during the day, and the father believes she had sex with them in front of Lisa.
- The father tried to resolve the problems several times, but as he put it, "The bottle won, and I lost."
- The mother in the first marriage (Jean) and Bill had totally different views on child rearing. Bill was more structured and organized, but nurturing and loving. Jean was more permissive, chaotic, and inconsistent. Much of her inconsistency of emotions may well have been connected to her alcoholism.
- Part of the divorce settlement was that Jean would have Lisa on weekends. Thus, Lisa was living during the week within a well-organized and consistent environment, but on the weekends, she was in a very chaotic setting.

The "new family" that was emerging contrasted greatly with the prior family environment. Bill and Karen got along well and complemented each other nicely. Karen was very supportive of Bill and Lisa, and Lisa seemed to really enjoy her. This harmony, however, was under stress from the fallout of the prior family dynamics. Lisa, we were to find out later, was having tantrums and emotional trauma at home as well as at school. While Bill and Karen had a new, more stable environment, Lisa was still experiencing two different worlds—one during the week

143

and another on the weekends—and this was creating personal turmoil.

## Helping Insights

Staff observations of Lisa's continued emotional outbursts, withdrawal, and masturbation provided the basis for team discussion and planning. Initial inquiries with the father brought only a firm denial that anything was wrong. "She is just going through a transition to school," he said. "She'll get over this!" But it was obvious that he knew that Lisa was really struggling with some deep emotional problems. He was very nervous and seemed to want very badly for things to settle down. Was Lisa having similar problems at home? "Well, somewhat," he said, "but not serious," and he was sure she was making the adjustment to school and things would get better.

Things simply got worse. Lisa was now beginning to mimic sexual activity for other children. A second conference provided more information. The father now explained that the divorce was more chaotic than he had originally said and that maybe this was causing some of Lisa's behavior. We assured him that we were there to help and that our concerns were that Lisa had some very serious emotional problems. He did not agree and started to blame the teachers, but held back. He did share that Lisa was having some of the same difficulties at home. We could sense that there was more to the situation than he was sharing, but his look of being emotionally drained told us to go slowly, to build trust through empathy and patience. At the close of the conference, he agreed to allow us to have a trained psychologist observe Lisa during school. He was pleased that we were concerned, and yet his nonverbal communication was filled with anxiety and anger.

A third conference was arranged shortly after the psychologist had completed several observation periods of Lisa. At this conference Bill's new wife Karen attended for the first time. It was obvious that she was "holding" things together for the new family through her very supportive relationships with Bill and Lisa. She was a good listener and had an unusual ability to grasp the key difficulties of a situation. Bill was still defensive and appeared ready to jump on us as a staff at the least provocation. We shared the results of the psychologist's observations. They were that Lisa was suffering from very deep emotional trauma related to some basic relationship conflicts most likely within the family and that possibly she had been sexually abused. The father, of course, was upset and said he did not think Lisa was disturbed that much and that we were over-reacting. His wife then intervened and asked him to share the whole story. "There is a problem, Bill," she said. "Explain to them what is behind this, we need to begin to help Lisa!"

He then explained all that had gone on in the previous marriage: the alcoholism, the sexually inappropriate behavior of the mother, and the very stressful conflicts that ultimately led to the divorce. He also explained that Lisa was still seeing her mother on weekends and that the situation was not good. The stepmother explained that they, too, had observed Lisa's symptoms increasing—the tantrums, the withdrawal, and the masturbation. She noted that these symptoms picked up right before the weekends (which is when Lisa went to see her mother) and right after the weekends. Things settled down a little during the main part of the week, when Lisa was on a good schedule. They both explained that they had met with the mother, but it was to no avail as she denied doing anything inappropriate in front of Lisa. Yet they were sure that the weekends were chaotic and very dominated by the mother's alcoholism and boyfriends.

By this point Bill was crying and Karen was consoling him. We were empathetic and offered to meet at another time if that would help. But Karen wanted us to continue, and Bill nodded his agreement. "What had the psychologist recommended?" Karen asked. "We need to act now as I can see that this situation is really going to have terrible effects on Lisa!" We shared with them that the psychologist suggested that Lisa participate in a play-therapy group that she was directing at the counseling clinic and that the entire family participate in a family-therapy process. At this point Bill lost control emotionally and screamed that no one needed therapy and that as far as he was concerned the conference was over! He left in a very distraught state. Karen explained that he was very anguished over this situation. She would talk with him once he settled down and get back with us. She thanked us for our help and assured us that she would get back with us.

Two days later, she called and said they had agreed that Lisa should be in the play-therapy class and that they would meet with the psychologist to at least discuss the possibility of family therapy. This was the breakthrough that made the difference for everyone in the family. While the biological mother never did participate in the process, she finally agreed to change her way of functioning when Lisa was with her on weekends. Lisa progressed with amazing healing. The play therapy allowed her to act out many of her conflicts in a nonthreatening environment. Within weeks the masturbation disappeared and the tantrums were subsiding. She still withdrew, but now accepted comforting from one of the teachers and was beginning to stay in "group time" longer each week.

Family therapy allowed the "new family" to clear the air and to establish some predominantly positive themes as related to their relationships. Bill in particular was able to put things into perspective and become more relaxed in his role as father. His love for Karen was solidified and his relationships at work became more relaxed.

Karen was a major force in helping both Lisa and Bill overcome the trauma of the previous family dysfunction. Through professional therapy and family nurturance of each other, Lisa is emerging as a very creative and happy child. The family is building new rituals that are solidifying their love and articulating the stress that has haunted them from the previous family system.

The teachers and other staff members noted the following suggestions as "helping insights" they felt were critical in their support of the entire family.

- Observe daily the child's behavior for needs and strengths.
- When a problem exists, get the family involved immediately.
- Show compassion for the family's situations and feelings.
- Involve other appropriate professionals in the resolution process.
- Reward and praise family members for even small gains they make in addressing the problem.
- Make essential adjustments in the classroom to accommodate the changes in the child's behavior.
- Maintain a confidential and empathetic relationship with the family.

## BLIND ANGER: A DETERMINED/CARING MOTHER

This case represents a set of family and community dynamics that fostered antisocial personality behaviors in a very young child. Three-year-old Mike was the most violence-prone child any of the staff had met. The case took place in a university child-care center in a medium-size city. It provides many insights on the complexities of families who have visible handicaps, little support, and a past history of negative experiences with formal social service and community agencies.

### The Context

Perhaps the first sign that Maria Blake had her "barrier" up to protect against the outside world was the way she completed the center's admission forms. Every form was completed with "Ms. Blake," never with a first name. In the orientation conference, the tone was just as formal, with no nurturing or partnership overtures. The family had been referred to us as badly in need of child-care and family assistance. The mother was polite, but very formal. What follows is a synthesis of information on the family that emerged ever so slowly over the three years that it was involved with the center.

Ms. Blake was the 30-year-old mother of Mike and Elsa (who was 12 years old at the time). She was technically blind, although she could see shadows of people and things up close. Elsa, the oldest child, was mentally handicapped and functioned at about the mental age of a six-year-old. Mike was intelligent, but was already showing signs of antisocial personality syndrome. Elsa was passive, compliant, and heavily influenced by peers. Mike was just the opposite; he was active, insightful, and quite independent.

The family was receiving assistance from the State Office of the Deaf and Blind and from the Department of Social Services. Social Services was suspicious of the family's economic situation as staffers believed that a man was present off and on in the family, but could never prove it. In spite of apparent poverty, the family never gave indications of lacking anything. Indeed, we were to learn later that the mother had a financially well-off boyfriend who did visit often. Her former husband had been quite abusive and may have caused brain damage to the oldest child. Apparently, he was currently in prison for a life sentence for killing a manager of a convenience store. We never knew the full situation as the mother avoided discussing this topic with us and with Social Services. The main thing that was known was that until about a year ago, the family lived in a violent and abusive setting.

The violence that family members had lived with still permeated their individual and group interactions. Social Services told us that the police had been called to the house several times to settle things down. Ms. Blake would get out of control and hit the children and get into a screaming fit. Neighbors would call the police, and the police would come and calm things down. This scenario repeated itself many times. Ms. Blake was distrustful of any outside person or group except for

148

one person who befriended her at church. Fortunately, this person (Mary) took an interest in the family and tried to help family members develop more positive ways of relating to each other. However, the overriding distrust of the outside world remained, and the violent behavior cycled through family relationships quite often.

Ms. Blake did not work, but did some volunteer work at the church (only when Mary would go with her). She wanted the two children to have the very best and pursued their interests with great energy. A real strength was her interest in seeing to it that the children were treated positively by others and received full recognition at school. While she was concerned about the children, her style of relating to them was mostly cold, distant, and punitive. Her own experience with abuse had tainted and distorted her idea of relating to others, especially to the children. She was also very externally oriented, always seeing the cause of her problems in some person or group external to her and the family. Ms. Blake was under constant medical care, but her illness was controlled through medication. She depended on others for transportation and emergency assistance.

The man that often visited Ms. Blake was machismo and a poor role model for Mike and Elsa. Unfortunately, he visited often and would overstimulate the children, especially Mike. He drank heavily and used drugs and would then become abusive with Ms. Blake. He would give the children money and any things they might desire. He literally caused chaos, and it would take the family two or three days to recover. At the center we could tell when he had visited as Mike's aggression would increase greatly.

There was also an intense racial hatred for white people in Ms. Blake and in her boyfriend. Apparently, she had been badly treated by white people in her younger years and had never resolved this hatred. Naturally, this hatred had penetrated the lives of the children and was carried over into their school relationships.

The home environment lacked literacy materials, but was filled with toys the boyfriend had acquired for the children. One positive thing was that Mary was beginning to bring books and other materials to the family. Mary played a major role in trying to help the family find more stability and harmony, although often her efforts were destroyed by a visit from the boyfriend.

This family had real problems emotionally and socially that were rooted in the mother's distrust, anger, and fear of other people. While her handicap limited her mobility with the children, her emotional dysfunction was the real barrier to the family's healthy functioning. It was a family of peaks and valleys, and Mike's behavior often reflected this cyclical process. Two hopeful features of the family's situation were the mother's strong interest in her children receiving a good education and Mary's friendship.

*Helping Insights*

Mike's first day at the center in the three-year-old classroom was filled with stress for everyone. He terrorized the room, pushing children over, throwing toys everywhere, and generally rejecting an otherwise orderly environment. He ended up spending most of the day in the director's office. It was clear that Mike could not function in a group setting at this point in his life. His style of relating to others was based totally on the use of physical and verbal abuse. He lacked the language and social skills for relating to the other children and to the teachers effectively. We called Ms. Blake to set up a conference, but she was ill and asked if we could come to the home. Two staff members went to the house for a home visit that day after school. Ms. Blake was sure that it was the teachers. "You have to be firm with Mike; let him know that he will be whipped if he does not behave properly," she said. The teachers explained that they did not spank children, but used positive discipline. "Not with Mike," she claimed. "You have to be clear on what he is to do and follow up with punishment."

Mike's behavior continued to be aggressive, abusive, and chaotic. He simply did not have the skills for functioning in a group. The other children were beginning to mimic his negative behaviors, and Mike was getting worse, not better. Further, the lead teacher in that room had little experience with such difficult behavior. She was reacting, instead of planning more systematic ways of trying to move Mike in more positive directions.

Within the week, the teaching team in the three-year-old room and the director of the center met to discuss and plan how to deal with Mike. We all agreed that we needed more information on Mike (at that point we did not know of the abusive family history). We also agreed that Mike needed much more individual attention of a nurturing nature and needed to have gradual experiences on how to function in a group. We needed to meet with Mike's mother, and we needed to somehow plan for more one-on-one experiences with Mike. We made arrangements for a conference with Mike's mother, who reluctantly agreed to come. Her friend Mary brought her to the conference and sat in on the conference at Ms. Blake's request. It was obvious that Ms. Blake did not trust us yet. At the conference we told Ms. Blake that Mike's language continued to be abusive and that just that day he had hurt two children on the playground. Was he this way at home? She said she was sorry that he was causing all of these problems. Yes, he could get out of hand at home. "But I hit him good and let him know he can't push me around like that," she said. "That teacher (who was white) is the problem. She has to really let Mike know who is in charge." The director explained that at the center only positive discipline was used and that the teacher was doing a good job of trying to help Mike. Ms. Blake was adamant that Mike could learn to behave properly and said she would talk with him. The director then explained that beginning next week Mike would be working one-on-one with an assistant teacher most of each morning. We want to help Mike learn how to feel good about himself, and we need your help at home. We need for you to reinforce the things we are doing during the day. Yes, she would do that, she said. She did not like the idea that Mike was not going to be in the group during the morning. "Nothing is wrong with him; he can learn to behave." We explained that this was temporary until Mike could learn to gradually adjust to the group.

The conference made several things clear. Mike was only used to abusive discipline; he had not experienced a loving relationship with his mother. In effect he was detached and did not have the warm, trusting feelings that many children experience in infancy and toddlerhood. It was also clear that Ms. Blake held a real distrust of anyone outside the home and had real racial hatred for white people. Her friend Mary had a child at the center, and so on another occasion, the staff asked Mary if she knew of the family's situation. "Yes," she said, "and it was a very difficult situation." She had tried to help and be supportive. There was an abusive husband who was now gone, and the current boyfriend was also abusive and disrupted the family greatly whenever he came. There was a lot of hitting and abusive language in the home. Ms. Blake can get violent with the children when she reaches her limit. She is frustrated because of her blindness and bitter about her life. But she can be a good person. Mary found her to be kind, but not warm, and usually negative. Mary assured the teachers that she would continue to do all that she could to help the family move toward more positive ways of living.

Progress was slow with Mike on learning social skills, but he did begin to explode with new language skills. The individual attention of having one person work with him in the mornings proved very beneficial. He was beginning to develop a positive self-image, and it was clear that he was capable of developing social skills when his energy was directed toward positive things. Some progress was also made with Ms. Blake. One staff member who Mike began to develop a relationship with agreed to be the key contact person with Ms. Blake. This was a breakthrough for the center as she accepted this teacher (mainly because of his ability to communicate with Mike). Each week the teacher visited with Ms. Blake in her home, and the two discussed how the week had gone for Mike and the ways they could work together to help Mike continue making small steps toward becoming more socially capable. These sessions also provided more information for all of the staff on the family's situation. For example, the teacher found out that during the night the older child would wake up Mike, and the two of them would then go downstairs and turn the television on. Ms. Blake had not been successful in getting them to stop this habit. The teacher talked with both of the children firmly, but in a positive sense. He instructed the older child to stop this habit and to use time during the day to play with Mike. He also told both of them that each week he would be spending time with them on how to get along, and that they would take a trip to eat each week. His positive, but firm, approach worked, and Ms. Blake was definitely impressed. She told Mary that the children were getting along better and that Mr. Cane was a good teacher. Some trust was beginning to emerge between Ms. Blake and at least one staff member at the center.

Mike's move to the four-year-old classroom meant that he would be with Mr. Cane every day. Their relationship strengthened, and Mike's behavior progressed markedly. He was now integrated into the group's daily schedule on a full-time basis, but still had individual attention through the efforts of Mary who spent four hours a week with him in the afternoons after naptime (which was a difficult period for Mike). With some positive events to look forward to, Mike began to see some of the positive aspects of life. He and Mr. Cane were becoming close friends, just what Mike needed. Further, his very positive relationship with Mr. Cane spread to his interactions with other teachers and to the children.

Mike still had his days of angry outbursts and aggression, but they were fewer and less intense. We had a psychology student who was highly skilled in behavioral problems observe Mike over an extended period and then work with us as a staff on specific strategies we could use to further the positive developments that Mr. Cane had stimulated. His observations confirmed our belief that Mike needed plenty of positive support activities, intense individual attention with nurturing but firm adults, and small group socialization opportunities. On this last suggestion, the student said that he noticed that Mike did well when he was with just three or four other children and for small periods of time. It was when Mike was in larger groups for long periods of time that he had real difficulties. He also noted that Mike still had real problems with authority figures other than Mr. Cane. We needed to involve Mike with other staff in activities that were success-oriented and to do so in a gradual manner, beginning with short time periods.

These suggestions were implemented and proved valuable in helping Mike improve his social skills. Another important thing that was happening with Mike was that he now was able to recognize when his behavior was getting out of control and would go to Mr. Cane and ask to spend time with him or be near him. This was a real step forward, and the staff was thrilled. Even though Mike would periodically slip backward and have a major tantrum, these episodes were fading.

The situation at home was also showing signs of small improvements. Mr. Cane talked with Ms. Blake's boyfriend when he was visiting the family. He asked him to stop the abusive language and drinking in front of the children. Although the man was initially upset, he did begin to behave more positively when around the children. There were still problems at home; Ms. Blake continued to have several anger episodes a week and had not really altered her negative and punitive approach to the children. Mr. Cane and the center director met with Mary and discussed the possibility of doing some parent-education activities in the home with Mary as a co-leader of the sessions. Mary agreed and suggested that this approach be prefaced with some positive feedback to Ms. Blake on how much improvement there had been in Mike. Mary also made an excellent suggestion: that we expand the circle to include another parent who lived close to both her and Ms. Blake, thus making the process more of a small group coffee-discussion time.

This strategy accomplished two things at least: it provided Ms. Blake with some very specific positive discipline activities she could begin trying out with Mike and the older child, and it expanded Ms. Blake's social network in a positive sense. The other parent was white, supportive, and was insightful about the hurt that Ms. Blake had experienced with other white people earlier in her life. It was a low-key, sharing and discussion time. The group met twice a month and began to do things informally with each other. Ms. Blake's new friend (Jean) offered to help her with transportation each Tuesday to the physician. We began to see a real change in the family through Mr. Cane's eyes. We also saw the effects on Mike in his more courteous behavior with adults at the center and in his interactions with other children.

Ms. Blake still had "authority figure" anger and would often call the center and vent her anger on the director. He was understanding of this process and was patient in responding to some difficult attacks. It seemed as if Ms. Blake was in need of hanging on to some anger as a buffer against the more positive things that were happening to her and the children. She would now apologize for her attacks two or three days later and explain that things just piled up and she needed to talk with someone. Gradually these "attacks" were fading and were replaced with more civil relationships with the center staff in general.

Mike still has problems, but his signs of antisocial personality syndrome are much less severe, and his overall approach to other children and adults is more positive. The gains came slowly and with a well-planned and positive approach to working and relating to Mike and the family. Ms. Blake, while still struggling with her anger and bitterness, had developed some new connections to the outside world through her friends Mary and Jean and through Mr. Cane. She has also gained some perspective on how her behavior affects the children and others. These insights are valuable because they provide the beginning points for longer-term progress. In a staff session devoted to reviewing "what worked best" in our efforts to develop a partnership with the family, the staff identified the following as helping insights that were learned and refined over a three-year period.

- Continually communicate a caring perspective with parents.
- Listen to the "sources" of the family's anger and not the surface bitterness.
- Be specific in communicating with parents on desired changes in behavior for the child.
- Create a "desired behavioral environment" for the child in the classroom.
- Offer specific parent-education opportunities, often nested within informal social and emotional support arrangements.
- Capitalize on any emerging staff-parent trust-building opportunities.
- Help bridge the family's movement to new situations.

## ADDITIONAL CASE NOTES AND HELPING INSIGHTS

The realities of the risks and barriers that all families face are immense and complex. They are not limited to the poor, to those who have the burden of severe physical handicaps, or to any single group in particular. The following are some observations about families who on the surface would certainly not be judged by most criteria as "at risk." Yet, as we share some of these situations, one can see the that factors such as "hurrying" parents and affluence can present enormous barriers to healthy development.

### Adulthood Now, Please

Because our culture is so success-oriented and because

parents receive so many mixed messages on the importance of the early years, some parents internalize a distorted view of what children should be like. One of the authors recalled the case of Mrs. Tram who symbolizes this syndrome of Adulthood Now, Please! Within the first week of school, Mrs. Tram was already pleading with the teacher to move on to academics and put the paints and clay on the shelves, please! Her daughter Belinda was fortunately an interesting and inquisitive child who wanted badly to get out from underneath all of the adult requirements being pushed her way. Energetic, creative, and very much a child (when the mother was not around, of course), Belinda struggled with the distorted perceptions of what her mother told her she should be. Indeed, Mrs. Tram was struggling but in a way that was confusing the child and herself. The intentions were good, but the direction was lethal.

Always dressed in clothes more suitable for a high school prom than for kindergarten, Belinda tried to be the adultlike child her mother seemed to want. Of course, it didn't work. It never really works because kindergarten children are not adults; they do not have the "program," so to speak, to fake it for very long. Yet, the conflicting expectations cause great risks. Perhaps the biggest risk is for a child to lose essential childhoodlike thinking and feeling. If we dress children like queens and kings and continually push them into adult roles, we can only expect that eventually they will get the message and put on the mask of being a sophisticated five- or six-year-old. How sad!

When Mrs. Tram failed to make headway with the teacher, she moved on to the program director. What was wrong with this program? She had heard good things and expected us to be teaching mathematics, reading, and some science. I explained to her that we were doing these things in ways that made sense to children and that helped them to experience the joy of learning. "Don't give me that stuff about play as learning," she said. "I want serious stuff going on in these classrooms." We spent literally hours discussing her feelings about what should be happening in school and about how we should be teaching. This was critical because it is the only way to open up avenues for finding some common ground that professionals and parents can begin to shape their trust and partnership. After about the third session with Mrs. Tram, it was noticeable that she was beginning to think about her position (I think this happened because we were thinking about our position, too!). Many of the other parents were happy with what we were doing, she observed. And Belinda loved school and was bringing home some very interesting projects. But she decided that Belinda needed more challenge for at least part of the day. Three afternoons a week, she explained, Belinda would be going to special enrichment courses offered by another school in the community. This was fine from our perspective, but I encouraged her to remember that Belinda was a child and not yet an adult and that she might want to talk with Belinda about this move.

We tried different approaches with parents who seemed in a hurry for children to grow up, particularly when this proclivity was in the extreme. We held lunchtime discussion sessions where parents and staff shared ideas about what was appropriate for young children at different ages. Sometimes we had guest speakers who addressed particular concerns of parents. Staff also photocopied articles and shared books on these topics. At least Mrs. Tram was open to discussion and reflection. Her most dramatic feedback came though from her daughter. Various stress symptoms began to appear (headaches, nausea, difficulty sleeping, weight loss, and mild depression). A complete pediatric health examination showed that Belinda had no physical illness. The pediatrician suggested that maybe Belinda was moving too fast with things. She seemed unhappy to him and under a lot of stress that was unnecessary. Little did the pediatrician know that his message matched ours and that his attention to these social and emotional aspects of Belinda's development was the "bell" that got Mrs. Tram's attention. Things began to change. Belinda was now back in the center fulltime every day. Mrs. Tram's visits with the staff were more directed toward Belinda's overall well-being. While she still struggled with her adult-oriented perceptions of how Belinda should function, we began to note changes for the better.

Not all parents "adjust" to the realization that children need a childhood. Some children suffer for a lifetime from not having this period of life where they can explore the many aspects of who they want to become. Parent education through conferences, group presentations, and study groups can promote some important thinking in parents and staff regarding what is really important during the early childhood years (Dimidjian 1989).

## Parent Obsessions with Physical Appearance/Sexuality

Children have a normal curiosity about their appearance and sexuality unless adults attenuate this aspect of development to the extreme. The authors have noted an increase in parental obsessions with this aspect of development over the past 10 years to an unhealthy level, for the child and the parent. Field notes on one such case are instructive regarding how this distortion can divert children from healthier ventures.

Ms. Sarin was a very outgoing person who was always willing to help at the school and showed real interest in Rene, her child in first grade. This interest, however, was focused to the extreme on Rene's physical appearance and sexual attractiveness. She dressed Rene in clothes that were not even appropriate for an adult and had obviously taught (through modeling mostly) Rene how to use her body to gain attention from others. Even the language she used to describe Rene was symbolic of her obsession with this aspect of development. "Rene is really sexy, don't you think?" she would say. Or, "I think Rene is going to have pretty breasts, don't you?" Mother's obsession (and in this case father's, too) in effect became Rene's obsession. While she avoided the use of overt language regarding her image of herself as a sex object, she often referenced her actions with overtures to this end. Naturally, some of the other children picked up on this obsession, and the first grade was soon preoccupied with sex and appearance. Through conferencing with Ms. Sarin and her husband, we were able to defuse the immediate problem in the classroom, but we were just as concerned that the process was still a major family focus at home.

Beauty contests, "dates," and women's magazines are not the "stuff" of young children's natural imaginary and real world. We conferenced several times with the parents, asking them to consider that Rene was just a child and needed time and space to explore her total development and interests. Indeed, at this early age of life, most children are more interested in learning to use their bodies for artistic and creative endeavors. Strong defenses went up in the parents, and they assured us that their intent was to help Rene achieve her full beauty—we simply misunderstood them. Again, Rene's ensuing emotional problems were the feedback that brought parental attention to their misconceptions of childhood. Her obsession with masturbation, exposing herself to other girls on the playground, and her mimicking of French kissing came like a bolt of lightning to the parents (and to some other parents who had children in the class). Behaviors once internalized are not reversed easily. In Rene's case, some play therapy and parental refocusing on what childhood is about provided the foundation for helping Rene focus on a healthy and total childhood. But important years were lost for Rene, and the "scars" will follow her through life.

Parental guilt, childhood obesity, and other family dysfunctions are often at the source of this obsession with physical/sexual appeal for their children (Bradshaw 1988). Our culture is also to blame. Television, cultural values, and many other daily messages are sent to all of us that weight, how we look, and how appealing we are to others are critical to our lives. Thus, every early childhood program should offer parents educational experiences where they can develop more balanced perspectives about the role of sexual development in childhood. It is also vital that we help parents and ourselves realize that children need to articulate their own identity and not an identity we might want for them. Our role is to nurture their interests and support them in their development by being whole and healthy role models. Parental obsessions with children's sexuality is just as abusive as any other form of child abuse. It distorts the child's filter of what is important in life (Erikson 1982).

## Rigidity and Overprotectiveness: Enemies of Growth

Being a parent is tremendously challenging. We have to learn to love in nurturing, not dogmatic, ways. We have to find "balance" in our relationships with children, protecting but not stifling them. We have to know about human development so we can interrelate with their need for us to let go at appropriate points, and for us to then intervene at certain points. Indeed, this is not an easy process. Perhaps the fears that so often penetrate our culture (high crime, increased rape, and other antisocial acts) have infected many parents with unhealthy doses of overprotectiveness and rigidity. It may be, too, that given the workload of young parents, they feel a strong need to "protect" and "schedule" children to the extreme. This problem can become a major risk factor for parents, children, and professional staff. Children need "room to grow" according to their stage of development and in line with their emerging personality (Caldwell 1989).

Mr. Feltin is representative of parents who overprotect to the point of damaging children. He's a single-parent father who is very sincere, but extremely rigid, in his approach to child rearing. Daily, he reminds the staff that Jimmy is not to get dirty, and that Jimmy should not be allowed to play with certain children. Staffers try to explain to him that getting a little dirty is just part of being five, and that Jimmy likes to play with all of the children. Yet, the father is adamant on these and other points of development. His rigid perspective and extreme protective focus is limiting Jimmy in harmful ways. Children need socialization with many different children, and they need opportunities to paint, play with water toys, and interact with the environment in natural ways—and this will bring on the dirt. We counseled with

Mr. Feltin and tried to gain his participation in programs we were conducting on child development and on parent-child relations. But he was always busy with work and assured us he knows what is good for Jimmy.

We eventually had a positive influence on Mr. Feltin (to Jimmy's great relief), but we were not able to help him relax a little more in his parenting style.

It is certainly true as research indicates that parents shape their style of parenting very early in their experiences with children. We need to reach parents early with supportive and reliable information on how important it is to attach to children and to become engaged with them, not manage them. Certainly we need to plan and organize orderly situations for children, but we must avoid cutting them off from the natural joys of learning and being with other children (Galinsky 1987).

## Some Final Insights

Parents can give children too much! It can become an obsession to give children everything they want in affluent homes. Children need to be challenged. They grow from having to imagine how they might fill particular needs that adults are unable to meet. Simplicity is what children use best in their inventive manipulations to create meaning where there is none. Filling every need for them is a barrier to their full development. Certainly we want them to have basic needs met and to be challenged through a stimulating, but balanced, environment. But toys upon toys and televisions in their rooms only rob them of their childhood. More than anything, children need parents who still have some "childhood" in themselves and are willing and eager to share it with their children. Too often we avoid counseling affluent parents on their obsession with giving to their children. We simply fail to see the risk in what they are doing. It is a shortcoming of our thinking. We tend to see "risk" as the more physically restraining factors in the lives of children. Yet spiritual poverty and "poverty of the loss of childhood" are the greatest of risks because they impinge upon the spirit of the child in each of us (Caldwell 1989). Racial and ethnic prejudices place all children at risk! In far too many cases, parents allow their own racially and ethnically distorted perceptions to infect their children's lives. This may show up in very subtle ways: putting children in homogeneous play situations, keeping them shielded from the richness of other cultural and racial settings, and limiting their literacy interests to only those that reference their culture. The roots of racism and ethnic prejudice are sown during the early childhood years. Early childhood professionals need to take the leadership in removing this barrier from the lives of children and in helping parents overcome their past limitations regarding cultural diversity. Play groups, classroom grouping-systems, placement of children on learning teams, parent-involvement strategies, school social events, and many other practices need serious review in light of the urgent need to address this barrier. Small parent-discussion teams, family cultural activities at school, and parent-sponsored multicultural reading activities are some examples of strategies every early childhood program can promote. Individual counseling of parents and children is also very critical during these formative years. In many ways this barrier reduces everyone's effectiveness in dealing with other barriers. Our learning materials, classroom practices, and school-family partnerships need to be assertive in promoting more multicultural environments (Powell 1989).

We are all at risk when children acquire distorted concepts of sex-role identity. This barrier of sex-role distortion has its sources in the very fabric of our cultural rituals. Boys should be aggressive; girls should be passive! Recent research on how math is often taught to girls is perhaps the most glaring educational deficiency in this regard. But there are others, such as the absolute obsession with sexuality in girls (which in effect creates an "object" of them and depersonalizes their human integrity) and the prevailing rigid alignment of affective roles for girls and instrumental roles for boys. Early childhood education offers the most promising opportunity to create healthy sex-role development in children. Parent education and counseling, equitable design of role expectations in the classroom, and the fostering of nurturing and problem-solving situations for girls and boys (in home and school) can stimulate the resolution of this tragic risk (Bronfenbrenner 1986).

Risks and barriers are not the property of any one element in our society. They are present in every family and represent the major roadblock to a strong and positive future in our society. The material presented here offers insights that can stimulate professional and parent thinking and action that will promote a healthier future. Beyond the professional-parent team, however, is the vast arena of our cultural community. As is evident in this material, communities must also reshape their approach to families and schools. A true human partnership must emerge if our society is to flourish.

# Chapter 5

# SUPPORTING AT-RISK FAMILIES: STRATEGIES THAT EMPOWER

Every attempt to strengthen families is a form of "strategy." Unfortunately, in many cases strategies are poorly conceived and isolated from the context of the child and family. They are often limited to one or two dimensions and unrelated to the needs and strengths of the children and families they are intended to help (Swick 1992). Effective child and family support strategies need to be based on an ecological framework and sustained through an empathetic approach. A major weakness in strategies that lack this foundation is their limited focus. Too often they attempt to resolve a "need" that is not fully understood and to do so with tools that are unrelated to the child and family context (Dimidjian 1989). An example of this limited approach is the use of the more is better syndrome. Children judged "not ready" (at risk) for grade promotion are given major doses of the very learning experiences that failed to meet their needs in the first place. Little or no analysis is carried out to gain a understanding of the learner's needs and little or no adaptation of instructional strategies is considered (Swick 1991b). The continuing failure of at-risk children throughout the early school years demonstrates that this generic approach is ineffective. An ecological-empathetic approach calls for a more comprehensive and viable system of support for children and families.

## THE ECOLOGY OF LEARNING: A STRATEGY PERSPECTIVE

The ecological approach to "strategy" has a predominant theme of inclusiveness. It requires us to be learners who are continually seeking ways that enrich and strengthen children, parents, and ourselves. In this process, our focus is on all of the possible influences and relationships that comprise the learning ecology: the child in interaction with family, school, and community; the parents in interaction with all of their contexts; and the teacher and "school" as they interact and develop an early childhood learning environment. Extensions of these dimensions of child, family, and school include the dynamic relationships among them as they interrelate to shape the major building blocks of society (Bronfenbrenner 1979, Garbarino 1982, Pence 1988, Ford and Lerner 1992).

The starting point for teachers and other early childhood professionals is to examine their "ecology of teaching and learning" as a strategy system. Too often this environment is not examined and is assumed to be a static part of the learning process. When it is examined, the approach used is often limited, focusing mostly on surface factors that are easily observed in the "system." Unquestionably, these assessments have produced some insight into the barriers to children's learning. However, for the most part, the results reflect the limitations of such an approach (Boyer 1991).

An inclusive approach, as is suggested by the ecological perspective, can probe the dynamics of teachers and schools in the early learning experiences of children and families (Swick 1991b). This approach asks questions like the following.

- What are teachers and schools doing to understand and influence the learning of at-risk children and their families during the preschool years?

- What "school entry" practices are being used to promote child and family success during this period of the family's life?

- How are teachers and schools relating to the cultural and learning-style differences present in children and families, particularly with regard to interpersonal, instructional, and curriculum factors?

- How are teachers and schools using proven practices such as peer teaching, mentoring, cooperative learning, and ungraded early childhood systems to promote a success orientation in at-risk children and their families?

- What are teachers and schools doing to design and use a caring-curriculum approach that incorporates concepts such as grandparents in the classroom, community-tutoring projects, intercultural exchange projects, and community-involvement projects?

Teachers and schools that reflect and act on the issues mentioned in the previous questions nurture the needed attitudes and behaviors for developing meaningful strategies. Failure to adequately probe the "teacher and school ecology" represents a limited strategy scheme and in some ways distorts the process of supporting at-risk children and families (Dimidjian 1989, Thompson and Hupp 1992).

Three very clear weaknesses in past approaches to teaching and supporting an at-risk child are: viewing the child out of context, relating to the child from a homogeneous perspective, and responding to the child's needs from a uniform position (Dimidjian 1989). Examples of this limited strategy perspective abound. You can find them in teachers' everyday comments, such as: "He lacks the maturity that the other children have," "Dana is just too active—she has a poor attention span," and "His language is just too different!" One might ask: Maturity in what sense? What is too active? When is language just too different? Developmental and ecological context knowledge, broadened perspectives about the learning styles of at-risk children, and the development of diverse ways of relating to children and families are framework strategies that increase the potential for helping children and families have successful school experiences (Swick 1991b).

Knowing what is an appropriate set of expectations for children at different stages of development is critical. Knowing the "range" of these developmental criteria and the diverse ways they can be expressed are essential strategy perspectives. Clearly, children must be able to carry out certain social skills within groups, but the degree of their viability to do so will indeed vary. Children should be active, inquisitive, and eager to interact in the environment. Our understanding of developmental context should inform us on how best to engage children in meaningful learning. No amount of elaborate activities or resources can mask the basic developmental need to search the environment for meaning. Similarly, the strong need in children for social and emotional attention will vary, yet in each child it is a need that must be accounted for in teachers' thinking and instruction (Erikson 1982). The child's total ecology must also be seen as significant to the creation of the early childhood program (Powell 1989). Children's family context, particularly their relationship with their parents, is an integral part of their emerging identity. Past approaches have too often ignored or given limited attention to the family as the primary learning environment (Comer and Haynes 1991). Understanding the family's learning orientation, prevailing relationship patterns, and strengths and needs is just as important as understanding the child's development. Family values, unique situations, special talents, and critical needs are "ecological context" that should influence teacher thinking and planning (Ascher 1988). In a very real sense, early childhood educators are "family educators" because whatever influence they have on the child is carried into the family. As at-risk families confront multiple problems in their lives, teachers become vital support persons (Pence 1988).

Another element in this ecology is the parent. Understanding the parent perspective is instructive with regard to the strengths, needs, and relationship patterns of the family. How do parents relate to their children? What self-image indicators are evident in parent behaviors? What do parents see as their most critical needs? What learning and educational interests of parents can be nurtured? These and other questions need to be integrated into the teacher's strategy efforts (Powell 1989).

The dynamics of the child's experiences within the family-school relationship shape their attitude and involvement

168

patterns (Swick 1992). Teacher assessment of this ecological process is vital to the teacher's continuing efforts to create learning activities that are meaningful to the entire family. Is the family-school relationship positive and supportive? Is it a collaborative process where the two contexts interact in shared ways? Are there times and places where family and school meet to plan and act on their common mission? Is the relationship a responsive and flexible one (Cochran 1988, Powell 1988, Schaefer 1985)?

In particular, the parent-teacher relationship sets the stage for how family-school and child-parent-teacher experiences emerge (Rich 1987). Research suggests that in the case of many at-risk families, this relationship is not nurtured by teachers or by other helping professionals (Ascher 1988). Cultural, social, and educational differences between parents and teachers often go unexamined, thus promoting an unnecessary barrier. Close scrutiny of this critical relationship should include questions like: What are my perceptions of the parents I work with? What are the bases of these perceptions? What are "parent priorities" in terms of what they are looking for in their child's teacher? How are parents and teachers communicating with each other? What types of invitations do parents get to participate in various ways in their children's education?

Understanding and acting on the family as a learning-system perspective is the foundation for creating supportive relationships with at-risk families. The child's developmental position, family ecology, parent context, teacher and school dynamics, and family-school relationships combine to create a "meta-strategy" that influences all of the elements of the early childhood program. Failure to account for any of these elements weakens the support role the early childhood educator plays in relating to families.

## AN EMPATHETIC APPROACH TO STRATEGY

An historical commitment to the teacher-as-helper

paradigm exists in the early childhood field. While the traditional emphasis has been on helping the child, recent efforts have highlighted the "family-support role" inherent in the early childhood profession (Swick 1991a). This family-support emphasis is emerging as an instructional strategy that can empower parents, children, and teachers. Further, the helping role is acquiring a broader conception in that it is being viewed as an interactive, a sharing, and a mutually participative process. An empathetic orientation is evident in practices such as mentoring, coaching, teaming, and participatory planning (Spacapan and Oskamp 1992). These practices appear to have a common emphasis on developing empathetic relationships with children and families. They are based on three very critical processes: teachers who take the role of empathetic helper, environments that expect and support positive learning, and strategies that promote a shared learning philosophy (Cataldo 1987; Dunst, Trivette, and Deal 1988; Galinsky 1988).

As noted earlier, the core of being an empathetic helper is in the process of seeking a better understanding of oneself as helper and of parents and children as growing persons. Combined with the ecological perspective, the teacher-as-helper emphasis alters the dynamics of the family-school relationship toward a more proactive focus. Teacher-as-helper emphasis promotes:

- more inclusive relationships among parents, children, and teachers
- increased sensitivity by parents and teachers to each other's situations and needs
- more preschool family-school interactions through parent education, child-development programs, and family-support activities
- increased parent roles and participation in planning and guiding the school's destiny
- more learning activities that use school and home as an arena for promoting children's school success.

Expectations and the support provided to achieve them are more symbolic of strategy than any other actions that take place in schools (Comer and Haynes 1991). It is not enough (but certainly a prerequisite) to expect all families to be learners and proactive. Strategy also requires visible supports within the school: a place where parents can get help, activities that encourage parents to be teachers and learners, artifacts that exhibit a respect for the cultural and individual values of families, policies and procedures that reflect the philosophy that families are valued, and a success focus that rewards family and child achievements (Rich 1987).

Shared learning experiences promote "empathy" and foster empowerment in family-school relations. Here again, the substance of strategy is in how this process of sharing and learning together is viewed and enacted. A true sharing process begins in shaping a mission together, one in which the parental perspective is a centerpiece of the professional's thinking. This involves both the professional and the parent in rethinking their ideas on how to work together. It also involves the development of activities that engage them in mutual efforts to create quality learning environments. Following are some examples of how schools and families carry out this shared learning approach. They

- help each other establish conditions where there is regular time to listen and learn from each other
- participate in training and other learning activities together
- develop and use decision-making policies that promote a partnership approach to solving problems
- conference in ways where perspectives are shared and where knowledge and strategies that empower families to be good role models for children are promoted
- foster in each other the guidance and mentoring roles so critical to children's development and learning.

171

# STRATEGIES THAT EMPOWER

Extensions of empowerment perspectives that strengthen families include engaging in community efforts that create better places for families, developing family-oriented programs in schools, advocating and supporting the development of quality preschool programs, designing and offering meaningful parent-education programs, organizing school-entry policies that promote child and family success, using success-oriented teaching practices, and carrying out individual teacher practices that empower children and parents.

## Advocating for Family-Centered Communities

One of the most critical, yet unattended, roles of the early childhood educator is empowering communities to seek environments that are family-friendly. Learning and development occur within all of the systems that impact children and parents as well as teachers (Hamburg 1992). Health, safety, enrichment, literacy opportunities, and meaningful work opportunities are heavily influenced by what citizens do in supporting these services. In a sense, at-risk communities create conditions that erode the integrity of families and schools (Swick 1991b). The following are examples of roles and actions that early childhood educators can pursue (Schorr and Schorr 1988).

- Serve on community-advisory teams that have opportunities to develop family-support programs and services.

- Advocate child-safety measures, such as safer playgrounds, supervised after-school and summer programs, better child-protection policies and practices, and improved neighborhood crime-prevention strategies.

- Initiate collaborative community-school activities, such as health and wellness days, immunization-awareness activities, family appreciation/support projects, and interagency parent-education.

172

- Promote community support of health and nutrition practices that reach all children and families in the community.

- Advocate improved literacy and job-training programs, particularly for parents in at-risk situations.

- Team with churches and civic groups to provide education and comprehensive support services to first-time parents, especially to very young at-risk parents.

- Encourage business and industry to develop family-strengthening policies, such as flextime, adequate maternity/paternity leave, child-care support services, and substantive benefits packages.

No matter how small, each community activity that empowers families is a preventive and enriching force that ultimately improves everyone's lives. Early childhood educators have a special challenge and a special opportunity to mentor their communities toward more responsive and supportive practices with regard to children and their families. Ernest Boyer (1991, p. 6) says it well:

> Clearly, when it comes to helping children, a balance must be struck. No one imagines returning to a romanticized version of the isolated, self-reliant family. Nor is it realistic to assume that a flurry of new government initiatives can do it all. The time has come to move beyond the tired old "family versus government" debate and create a new network of support, a new kind of extended family—at once both reliable and compassionate, a special blend of public and private services for children.

## Parent Education

A significant element of this new agenda for families is parent education. Schools can no longer wait until children come to school to have relationships with parents. Parents need knowledge, support, linkages to the community, and avenues for growing even before the birth of the first child. Many public schools are now offering parents preschool child-development programs and expanded early childhood services like "extended day" and summer enrichment. These family services offer a starting point for creating special parent-education efforts. These parenting programs need to initially focus on the developmental and personal experiences of parents (Powell 1989). In effect, parents need to set the direction in the sense that they are able to meet personal needs through these experiences (Cowan and Cowan 1992).

Ellen Galinsky (1987), for example, suggests that initial parent-learning experiences emphasize the nurturing, teaching, and modeling roles as they are formed by parents during the early childhood years. As emphasized by Galinsky, the need is for parents to "image" themselves as caring and worthy persons. Without strong and positive self-esteem, parents are limited in their efforts to empower their children. Swick (1991b, pp. 53-54) notes:

> Exemplary early family and parenting support-programs are focused on the critical element of the parent as nurturer. Whether these programs or practices occur in hospitals, churches, civic centers, or elsewhere, they need to create conditions in which parents can successfully explore their initial images of themselves as capable of spiritual and emotional growth through parenthood.

Parent-child centers and family resource-centers are two approaches that lend themselves to collaborative arrangements between schools and other groups. Many different services (e.g., home visits, parent drop-in activities, family counseling, group-training sessions) can be integrated into such centers. Within such centers particular services can be organized for meeting the needs of at-risk families. The emphasis in supporting at-risk families can be preventive, and yet focus on helping parents

174

resolve stressors like drug abuse or illiteracy and on assisting them in gaining control over their lives. Following are some of the basic elements that need to be included in these designs.

- Help parents acquire resources to meet basic family needs (e.g., housing, food, clothing, health care).
- Support parents in their efforts to acquire needed life skills, such as literacy and job training.
- Engage parents in actions that help in resolving at-risk conditions, such as illiteracy and social problems.
- Help parents gain needed information and skills for strengthening their understanding of children and themselves.

A natural extension of parent education should be the support of parental efforts to better carry out the parent-as-teacher role. Parents need to be involved in the planning of these experiences. Early childhood educators and parents need to see each other as partners in this growth process (Pence 1988, Powell 1988, Rich 1987, Schaefer 1991). One example of this positive and shared approach is the Family Literacy Project (Darling 1989). This project attempts to improve the education of at-risk families by going beyond the confines of the classroom. It provides early intervention to break the cycle of illiteracy through a combination of quality early childhood education for preschool children, and parenting and adult education for parents. This strategy uses several components: adult education, parent education, family services, vocational development, and early childhood development. A strong element in the program is that parents are involved with their children in the learning process, while also acquiring skills that can strengthen them as adults and parents (Darling 1989).

Home visits, group meetings, family-support centers, parent networking, and parent-training sessions offer multiple strategies for involving parents in acquiring knowledge and skills so critical to family empowerment. Swick (1992) found that trained home-school workers were effective in delivering "parent-child home-learning activities" to parents of at-risk children in the kindergarten and primary grades through the home-visit process. Participation in the home visits was high, with parents also increasing their involvement at school. Success with this strategy is enhanced when home visitors establish a supportive relationship with parents, parents are clear on their roles and supportive of the project's focus, visit times are flexibly scheduled, and other strategies are used to supplement the visits.

Group meetings, when designed to be responsive to family needs, can be effective in engaging at-risk families in shared learning and social support activities. Powell (1988) noted that small group parent-meetings provide the context for discussion, sharing, clarification of ideas, relationship building, and active learning. They are not the place for lecturing or solving sensitive individual problems or family problems. Further, some parents are not ready to actively engage in small group meetings; their concerns may be at an individual level that require more one-to-one interaction with the parent educator (Powell 1988). Large group meetings are best used for specific information functions. Training sessions should capitalize on existing parent skills in creating a climate where parents both learn and share with other parents. In too many instances, training programs are dominated by professionals, losing the needed self-esteem energy present in parents. The active involvement of parents in using newly acquired home-learning activities with other parents in role-playing situations stimulates more parent interest in mastering and applying these skills (Rich 1987).

Family-education centers are emerging as a new way for schools to establish a continuing effort to empower families (Swick 1991b). Such "centers" are typically housed as a part of the school's early childhood program and combine many services under the family-empowerment umbrella. Services often include parent education, adult-education support services, family-specific assistance, family-referral services, parent clubs, home-help hot lines, and a variety of related services. In many cases these centers serve to stimulate and engage parents in using "preventive services" to prepare their children and themselves for school success (Powell 1989).

Parent networking as supported by schools and communities is proving to be a creative way of encouraging families to develop strong support systems that strengthen their family potential for responding to stress (Cochran and Henderson 1990). In this scenario, parent clubs or other parent-directed groups organize to help each other deal with challenges and interests they have in common (Cochran 1988). The issues will vary according to the developmental and ecological needs of parents and families, but the processes of sharing, collaborating, and supporting are consistent across the functioning of networking-oriented groups.

Comer and Haynes (1991), Rich (1987), and Swick (1991b) identify a plethora of other strategies that can be effective in reaching parents and families in at-risk situations: conferences, home-learning activities, periodic parent notes, home-lending libraries, communication activities, advisory groups, classroom-volunteer programs, and related strategies. Regardless of the particular strategy, parent education and family strengthening are only as effective as families and schools make them. This calls for a new conception of parent-teacher partnerships, particularly with regard to meeting the needs of at-risk families.

Swick (1991b, p. 117) describes the substance of this new parent-teacher partnership in the following.

Together, parents and teachers need to conceive of their partnerships as growth-oriented experiences in which they seek to nurture each other toward becoming full partners in their support of children's learning and development. In this empathetic approach, teachers and parents must begin their journey with high regard for each other, their children, and the partnership they are seeking to develop. This calls for seeing each other as capable people, for listening to each other in responsive ways, and for nurturing each other toward the full realization of our talents.

## *Preschool Programs That Strengthen Families*

Whether sponsored by schools or collaboratively with other agencies, quality preschool programs are a powerful force in the lives of families. Indeed, there is considerable evidence that quality preschool and early education have a transforming influence on at-risk families. Garbarino (1982), Pence (1988), and Powell (1989) suggest that exemplary programs engage parents and children in experiences that generate lifelong habits among family members, habits that support child and parent success. Schorr and Schorr (1988, pp. 192-200) synthesize two decades of research that highlight the empowerment potential of this strategy (see Figure 5.1).

### Figure 5.1
### Impact of Quality Preschool

Reduces
- School Failure
- School-Dropout Rate
- Special Education Placements
- Delinquency Rates
- Welfare Dependency
- Teen-Pregnancy Rate

Increases
- School Readiness
- Completion of High School
- Post High School Education
- Employment Potential
- Proactive Behavior
- Economic Productivity

Child success in preschool appears to also stimulate some very positive behaviors in parents: parents take more interest in their children, become more positive toward them, are more involved in literacy activities, talk with them more, attend to their own education more, and actualize more proactive family rituals, such as reading and mealtime discussions (Pence 1988, Powell 1989).

178

These positive influences occur more often in high-quality programs. Programs that neglect child development needs and ignore the family may actually impede the integrity of at-risk families. The following are indicators of quality preschool programs.

- highly trained early childhood staff
- low teacher-child ratios
- safe physical environments
- interesting learning experiences
- nurturing adult-child interactions
- strong parental involvement
- well-equipped settings
- professional status and support for staff
- stimulating and appropriate curriculum

Programs with these attributes have been advocated by teachers as one of the major ways to empower at-risk children and their parents (Boyer 1991).

Unfortunately and tragically, children are not typically the recipients of such care. While quality preschool education is most needed for children and families at risk, they are least likely to receive it. Nationally, while 75 percent of children in families whose income is at or above $75,000 are enrolled in preschool, only 41 percent of children in families with an income of less than $20,000 are enrolled (National Center for Education Statistics 1991). Further, nearly 40 percent of children in out-of-home care are not protected by any state or federal regulations (Schorr and Schorr 1988). The situation that far too many children experience in preschool centers is described in an example by Boyer (1991, p. 60).

The atmosphere was chaotic. Doors were locked to prevent children from straying. One staff person "supervised" 10 three-year-olds in a room with few toys and a hard-surfaced floor. With a rapid turnover of hassled, demoralized, poorly paid and poorly trained teachers, the children were rarely

179

taught and seldom comforted. The directors were defensive. Outsiders were not encouraged to visit. Could parents have known what was happening here? Why should any child want to spend time at such a place?

As advocates and teachers of children and families, our efforts to empower must include the advancement of preschool programs through high-quality accreditation standards, teacher training, improved salaries, more family involvement, and more community support. High-quality preschool care combined with competent parenting are our two most powerful means of family strengthening.

## Supportive School Beginnings

Children and parents in at-risk situations need strong doses of success, especially as they embark on their journey in school. Kindergarten-primary programs should be especially sensitive to creating supportive environments for children as they begin school. Unfortunately, most school-entry practices focus on sorting children into groups, thus creating immediate stereotypical views of them, particularly with regard to their potential to succeed. As Hale-Benson (1986) notes, current procedures for school entry are quite frequently destructive of the children's self-esteem before they even have a chance to engage in meaningful school activities. Major changes are needed, with practices such as the following being used to support family and child success during the early school years.

- family-centered school-entry approaches where parents and children are encouraged to start off their child's education journey on the right foot

- comprehensive developmental and health assessment and supportive services that aim to assist children and families in reaching their full potential

- intensive and proactive teacher-parent interactions in which a positive family-school agenda is nurtured

180

- proactive strategies that address the specific learning needs of at-risk children and their parents in positive ways

- effective school-transition strategies where professionals and parents assure continuity of experiences for children

The initial experience of parents and children in school environments should be nurturing and caring. Teachers should learn as much as they can about the child and the family so that positive strategies can be used to create a foundation for school success. Parents need to be invited and encouraged to learn about the school, particularly about their child's teacher and classroom. The major emphasis of school-entry experiences for children, parents, and teachers should be that of empowerment (Dimidjian 1989).

Children's positive initiation into the school culture is best realized through two critical processes: positive teacher attitudes and the involvement of parents (Swick 1991b). Teachers who are proactive in their perceptions and relationships with at-risk families are more successful in engendering positive feelings and behaviors in children and parents (Slavin and Madden 1989). Involved parents generate a powerful success energy in children and teachers. Swick (1992b) suggests five teacher behaviors in this regard.

- Engage in shared learning experiences with parents where a success focus becomes the primary concern.

- Learn about parent and family cultural values and integrate these into the early relationships and activities with children and parents.

- Offer parents several different ways to get involved and provide supports that enable them to establish an involvement ethic.

- Engage parents right from the start in planning and managing children's early learning experiences with the school.

181

- Provide and pursue family-learning experiences (e.g., parent education, adult education, family reading) that focus on school readiness and success at the very outset of school entry.

## Success-Oriented Early Schooling

At-risk families often find themselves stereotyped within the school culture. They and their children are tracked and/or grouped into special classrooms and programs three times more often than others (Children's Defense Fund 1987, Hilliard 1976). They also repeat grades and are "over-age" for grade level more often (Boyer 1991). It appears that for many at-risk children and families, school becomes one more stressor within their already stressful environment.

Yet, it is the child and family who are in at-risk situations that need success in school as an antidote to their many challenges. Success-oriented schools and responsive teachers can be an empowering force in the lives of at-risk children and their parents (Rutter 1987). Quality early childhood programs need to focus on the total needs and ecology of the child and family. This means truly addressing the physical, medical, social, spiritual, and intellectual facets of the developing child and family. A success-oriented program does not assume that the basic needs of children and parents have been met. It continues to monitor and support the total growth process (Dimidjian 1989). It also creates continuity of school experiences across age and developmental levels.

There are several criteria suggested by researchers (Comer and Haynes 1991, Connell 1987, South Carolina Primary Success Design 1992, Rutter 1987, Slavin and Madden 1989) as guidelines for shaping school success programs.

- Maintain a strong emphasis on developing a positive self-image in the child and in the parent.

- Use diagnostic and developmental assessment strategies that support and promote the continuing development of the child and the family as a whole.

- Relate in positive and empowering ways to the total family system.

- Use diverse teaching strategies that nurture the distinct learning style of each child as it emerges within the family-school relationship.

- Apply an integrated curriculum approach that focuses on meaningful learning experiences.

- Use school-family curriculum activities that reflect a unified emphasis on language, math, and social learning skills.

- Organize inviting classrooms that use stimulating learning centers to engage children in exploratory activities.

- Apply inclusive grouping strategies that avoid tracking and promote a child-success philosophy in the classroom.

- Organize continuous progress, nongraded, multiage instructional systems that are success-oriented.

- Use assessments that are based on multiple interactions with the child and family.

- Create strong parent-teacher partnerships that focus on having a viable family-school system.

## TEACHER ROLES FOR EMPOWERING

Teachers' and care givers' potential influence on at-risk children and families is substantial. Purkey and Novak (1984) point to the invitations that teachers send (or do not send) to children and parents as critical to the creation of success-oriented learning. These messages are given through attitudes, relationships, expectations, human responsiveness, and in other ways. Rutter (1987) noted that positive teacher attitudes, well-planned instruction, and close teacher-child involvement escalated child achievement in school.

There are many things teachers can individually pursue to empower the family. They can begin with their focus on relating to the child's total well-being. Dimidjian (1989, p. 47) states:

> Whether early educators are working with a child of three or eight years of age, the basic tenet is to ensure that they view and educate each child as a developmental entity who needs appropriate placement in an early education setting where opportunities to learn are offered as developmental processes and where empowering adults interact to develop the child's mind, body, and social-emotional domains of personality.

She (Dimidjian 1989, p. 48) articulates this process clearly with regard to the perceptual focus early childhood educators should pursue.

> In working with family and child, the effective early educator maintains active empathy. If one succumbs to judging a child "bad" or a family "just no good," effectiveness crumbles. Empathy does not mean acceptance. Rather, empathy—the capacity to emotionally connect, to intuitively comprehend how someone else's behavior or even life has taken on a form so different from one's own—enables the teacher to maintain a teacher-parent relationship with a stressed or hard-to-reach parent.

An attitude of openness to the real problems children and families face and to using one's support system to relate to these challenges is integral to empathetic teaching. "Closed classrooms" assure that children will not get connected to needed sources of empowerment. They also lead to overwhelmed, and then often disenchanted, teachers. In effect, our work with at-risk children and families must be a team endeavor. The ecological nest of family life (and the potential resources therein) must be tapped. As professionals we are, as Dimidjian (1989) calls it, "developmental interaction specialists." She identifies 12 critical role strategies individual teachers can use in promoting child and family empowerment: observing, designing, facilitating, nurturing, exploring, guiding, informing, modeling, disciplining, assessing, referring, and teaming.

In correspondence with the concept of the match, teachers of at-risk children attempt to achieve synchrony among the roles to be emphasized and the needs of children and families being served. In other words, some children may need more guidance, while others may require strong health-care supports. The role-strategies are used with all children, but the needs dictated by particular risk factors may call for special emphases. For example, a child who is homeless will certainly need major nurturing and modeling of social skills as well as specific family-support services (Towers 1989b).

Each child and family needs individual attention as related to the application of these strategies. LeTendre (1990) notes that teachers need to expand their involvement through the roles of catalyst, broker, coordinator, coach, and others. Children's context and behavioral patterns vary, and thus their needs call for particular strategies. Child and family strategies that teachers have found useful in resolving different risk factors are as follows:

- providing the child with an adult mentor who can guide him or her academically and socially. This is particularly effective with children who do not have a father or who lack a stable parenting figure.

- connecting the parent to needed counseling services. This is especially needed in families where one or more adults are drug-addicted or where other abusive behavior patterns exist.

- linking children to needed speech and language therapy. More children than ever appear to be suffering from a lack of language-enrichment experiences.

- involving children in preventive tutoring programs that focus on one-to-one language development and reading-enjoyment activities, such as in the Reading Recovery Program.

- engaging parents in needed adult education and job-training activities. In some cases the need may be for courses to complete high school, and in other cases, the need may be for specific job skills.

- involving children in social-skills training activities, such as listening, sharing, communicating, and helping. This strategy is often interrelated with mentoring and home-learning activities.

- structuring the classroom to provide maximum levels of personal attention to children at risk (e.g., small child-adult ratios, assistant teachers, and the wise use of computer-assisted learning).

A framework for coordinating these and other strategies includes these five steps suggested by Dimidjian (1989, p. 52):

1. Obtain and use a child's developmental history to ascertain the interplay of internal and external factors that have contributed to the current difficulty as well as coping strengths in child, family, or community systems.

2. Identify current developmental delays or deficits as well as overall growth patterns, developmental strengths, or special gifts/skills.

3. Describe an individualized program of intervention and target goals and procedures for reaching these goals within a defined time frame.

4. Plan for ongoing communication and cooperation with parents and other adults in the child's educational and social environment.

5. Record regular observations of the child's changing behaviors to be used in periodic evaluations and conferences with parents and staff.

Early childhood teachers can make a significant difference in the lives of at-risk children and their families. Research has identified some key roles and strategies teachers and schools can play that function as protective and empowering influences. Benard (1992, p. 7) notes:

> The evidence demonstrating that a school can serve as a "protective shield to help children withstand the vicissitudes that they can expect of a stressful world" abounds, whether it is coming from a family environment devastated by alcoholism or mental illness or from a poverty-stricken community environment, or both.

Three particular empathetic strategies teachers need to emphasize are caring and support, projecting high expectations, and offering opportunities where children can find connections and meaning in their lives. These strategies can be achieved in various ways. Benard (1992) provides some examples related to the caring/supportive teacher reported in the research literature. One example is from Werner's (1987) Kauai study and deals with role modeling. Two elements are cited: "the teacher as confidante" and "the teacher as positive model." The caring and supportive teacher is indeed a source of power for many at-risk children. Whether it is through tutoring, special activities, or simply providing the child with daily encouragement, empowering teachers have a far-reaching influence.

Researchers (Rutter 1987, Edmonds 1986) found that teachers and schools that establish high expectations (and provide the support to achieve them) have very high rates of success. Within at-risk communities, some schools achieve far beyond others, and one of the determining factors is that they foster high self-esteem and promote social and academic success (Rutter 1987). Teacher strategies used in these successful schools include:

- clear, demanding, and challenging instruction
- positive and responsive relationships with the children
- supportive learning environments with multiple re-

sources to meet varying learning needs

- continuing communication with children that they can be high achievers
- strong family-involvement systems

High expectations must be matched with a plethora of opportunities for participation and involvement in the learning environment. Again, Rutter's (1987) research is instructive. He found that in schools with few problems, children were given a lot of responsibility. They participated very actively in all sorts of things that went on in the school; they were treated as responsible people, and they reacted accordingly. Teacher approaches to achieving this involvement process were to engage children in active learning roles, problem-solving situations, challenging curriculum, and cooperative learning and management roles (Slavin and Madden 1989). Further, teachers created classrooms where caring, sharing, and discussion were common to the culture of teacher and child relationships.

Family-oriented instruction has been noted as a major strategy for responding to the needs of children. A continuing stream of research has substantiated the significance of family-literacy habits and home-learning activities as highly successful instructional strategies (Swick 1991a, 1992). In addition to the critical teaching role parents play during the preschool years, the early school years offer many opportunities for parent participation. The following are some examples of family-oriented practices that have been effective (Swick 1991b).

- educating parents about the school's curriculum and articulating key areas where home-learning assistance is needed

- organizing home-learning modules for parents to use with their children to supplement classroom instruction

- carrying out home-visit programs that include parent education on key concepts the children are learning in school

- setting up family-learning centers (with books, magazines, and learning activities) in the classroom or school

- involving parents in various classroom- and school-support roles

- engaging parents in collaborative decision-making roles through various advisory and school-improvement groups

## TOWARD A FRAMEWORK FOR EMPOWERING AT-RISK FAMILIES

Early childhood education offers the best opportunity for responding to the needs of at-risk families in a comprehensive, sensitive, and supportive framework. The strategies and perspectives presented have focused on the use of an empowerment approach. This approach emphasizes the development of positive, preventive, and supportive means of strengthening children and families. In this framework, the needs and strengths of families are related to the overall development of family, school, and community systems that offer ways to strengthen the total human development process. The following is a synthesis of the key elements of a framework early childhood educators can use in their work to strengthen families. These elements include the philosophical basis, a proactive assessment system, collaborative planning ideas, prevention-oriented strategies, comprehensive community-support practices, and school-family strengthening activities. Teacher-parent leadership is the foundation in that it is this partnership that ultimately brings the empowerment process to reality.

### Philosophical Basis

The philosophy of the early childhood educator and the school is the basis upon which relationships with at-risk families evolve. This philosophy, as discussed throughout the book, should reflect an ecological-empathetic orientation toward families that aims to empower everyone involved. The three key elements are: ecology, empathy, and empowerment.

The ecological element references the need for an inclusive framework regarding school-family relationships. It calls for recognizing and including all of the aspects of the child-family system in the planning of strategies as well as all of the aspects of the school ecology and the interactive dynamics of the school-family system. Perhaps this element is best represented in the urgent need for a more protective social system for infants and young children from parental and societal practices that are abusive, neglectful, and ultimately quite destructive (Fontana 1992).

The empathetic element focuses on understanding and relating to families in positive and supportive ways. It calls for relating to families and ourselves from a perspective of strength, while also articulating and addressing needs that may be inhibiting the development of these strengths. The power of adult attitudes and values related to children and families is most indicative of this element (Caldwell 1989, Fowler 1989). The empowerment element is the process by which early childhood professionals and families enter into mutually supportive activities. The nature of these activities should evolve from a responsive and sensitive professional-family relationship. The basic premise is that families are growing, dynamic human learning systems that thrive on support and meaningful interactions with empowering early childhood teachers. Autonomy-promoting programs and practices, such as parent education, child care, and family-support projects are important indicators of this empowerment element (Powell 1989).

## Proactive Assessment

The true meaning of assessment is that to be able to enter into mutually responsive relationships, the collaborating parties must first come to an understanding of each other's contexts, needs, strengths, and goals. This process is best achieved early in the relationship and through sensitive, sharing, and supportive means. Teacher-parent visits, sharing of insights on each other's contexts and perspectives, and the articulation of the focus of their mission are essential aspects of this process. The use of comprehensive and growth-promoting sources of information (i.e., parent knowledge, teacher insights and observations, family history, developmental and health assessments) is important to creating a viable basis for continued productive school-family relationships. Empowerment requires a system of feedback by which families and schools (parents, children, and teachers) can challenge, support, and refine their attempts to grow and develop. It needs to be an anticipatory, preventive, and nurturing process where the learning partners are intent on helping each other achieve their full potential (Swick 1987, 1991b).

## Collaborative Planning

Perhaps the weakest part of school and community efforts to assist at-risk families is the lack of a truly collaborative relationship. The traditional mode of professionally dominated planning needs to be replaced with a more shared process in which all members of the school-family-community system are involved. Early childhood educators can begin this process very early in the family's life through both community and school efforts. For example, parent-education programs and related family-literacy projects can be initiated during the preschool years. A significant part of these early contacts with parents must be the involvement of professionals and parents on collaborative issues such as: What are the critical family and school needs with regard to children's development? What resources are essential to meeting these needs within the total system of the family? In what ways can early childhood professionals and parents engage in mutually supportive efforts to improve the human ecology for children and themselves? The communication tools of listening, observing, continuous sharing, responsive analysis, and teaming

191

are vital parts of this empowerment effort (Comer and Haynes 1991).

## Prevention Orientation

Healthy families are able to resolve most risk factors because they have internalized empowering beliefs and actions. The prevention of risk contexts and behavior patterns is best realized through parent- and family-strengthening strategies carried out during the family's formative period. Prenatal health care, literacy acquisition, nurturing family-relationships, competent parenting, and economic viability are elements of what might be called the healthy family syndrome. These preventive family-strengthening patterns should be integrated into the early childhood professionals planning efforts. In effect, child-development centers, early education programs, teachers, and other support staff should think prevention when engaged in planning. An empowerment process attempts to shift human energy from constant reactive activities toward proactive and strengthening activities. The simple realization that proper prenatal care and consequent reductions in low-birth-weight newborns does in fact increase the power of child and parent is an example of this approach. New and more client-directed educational and action strategies need to be explored with the intent being to create a prevention mentality throughout our culture (Albee 1992).

## Comprehensive Support

The needs of families in general and particularly those in at-risk situations dictate that early childhood professionals provide comprehensive programs. Again, these efforts need to be life-spanning in design, with the emphasis on prevention during the critical early years and carried out within interagency, community-wide systems. Planning frameworks need to envision large-scale efforts inclusive of neighborhood and community security, enrichment opportunities for families as well as more traditional services like parent education, health care, quality schooling, and social supports. Each community needs to be involved in this effort; it is too critical to leave to one or two groups to confront. Given the economic, social, educational, and "community building" factors involved, it is realistic to envision early childhood community planning teams at work on this task (Hamburg 1992).

## School-Family System

Ultimately, early childhood programs can empower children and families best when the strategy framework is based on a school-family system design. This system, of course, must be "nested" within healthy community contexts. Sporadic family-involvement activities are useful but limited in their long-range influence. The focus of a systems framework is on establishing and maintaining a continuing relationship with families. Included in such designs are goals shaped by parents and teachers, success-oriented early schooling practices, multiple parent-involvement avenues, and a school-home curriculum emphasis (Rich 1987).

## EMPOWERED FAMILIES AND SCHOOLS

Three particular observations are useful in summarizing the thematic emphases of this book: the ecology of at-risk children and families can best be strengthened through empathetic school and community efforts; early childhood professionals are most effective in empowering at-risk families when they are understanding of the true needs of families and of their own strengths and roles in being family helpers; and support structures for at-risk children and families must evolve from the collaborative efforts of parents and early childhood professionals.

Empathetic approaches to supporting at-risk children and families are having an empowering influence. For example, Benard (1992) notes that positive teacher attitudes and a challenging and supportive school environment do influence

193

children's social and academic behavior in positive ways. It has also been noted that well-designed parent education has helped to increase parent self-confidence and that quality early childhood programs have increased the family's total viability (Gordon 1975, Pence 1988, White 1988). The distinguishing feature of programs that have a positive influence is the empathetic, nurturing orientation of professionals toward families (Powell 1989). Their sensitivity, warmth, responsiveness, and general competence greatly influence parent and child participation, sustained involvement in activities, attitudes and behaviors, and desired program processes and outcomes (Garmezy 1992, Slavin and Madden 1989).

Empathetic professionals exhibit self-understanding and insights relative to the contexts and potential of the families they serve (Caldwell 1989, Edelman 1992). These early childhood professionals have an empowering influence because they recognize the mutual and reciprocal nature of the learning and development process. They support this process by using three critical strategies: developing a positive and proactive self, acquiring an understanding of the strengths and realities of the parents and children they serve, and focusing on autonomy-building strategies in their relationships with families (Swick 1991b). In effect, they empower through the sensitive use of self-concept enhancing strategies.

Supportive efforts and resources must be shaped collaboratively where parents and professionals jointly develop their empowerment agenda. As Comer and Haynes (1991) and Powell (1989) note, successful early childhood family-oriented programs use various approaches to involving parents and children in developing and carrying out support and family-strengthening activities. They are engaged in shaping their destiny and in creating skills for becoming more autonomous and for taking on new leadership skills. The collaboration process is based on an equality of relationships where parents and professionals attempt to share and learn from each other. High regard, continuous communication, and a mutuality of concern for growing through partnership are the distinguishing features of this process (Swick 1991b). The larger community system must be an integral member of the collaboration structure, providing enriching and enabling opportunities through quality health care, safe neighborhoods, productive educational systems, and other sustaining services. Perhaps most importantly, communities need to provide a sense of human dignity through community solidarity that says to families they are the most valuable resource in the ecology (Hamburg 1992).

The realization of every person's potential is the global goal of truly empowering early childhood education. It is through sensitive, empathetic, comprehensive, and collaborative school-family-community efforts that this goal can be achieved.

# REFERENCES

Albee, G. 1992. Saving children means social revolution. In *Improving Children's Lives: Global Perspectives on Prevention,* G. Albee, L. Bond, and T. Monsey. (eds.). Newbury Park, Calif.: Sage.

Albee, G., Bond, L., and Monsey, T. (eds.). 1992. *Improving Children's Lives: Global Perspectives on Prevention.* Newbury Park, Calif.: Sage.

The Annie E. Casey Foundation. 1992. *Kids Count Data Book: State Profiles of Child Well-Being.* Washington, D.C.: Center for the Study of Social Policy.

Anastasiow, N. 1988. Should parenting education be mandatory? *Topics in Early Childhood Special Education* 8 (1): 60–72.

Ascher, C. 1988. Improving the school-home connection for poor and minority urban students. *Urban Review,* 20: 115–21.

Baumeister, A., Kupstas, F., and Klindworth, L. 1992. The new morbidity: A national plan of action. In *Saving Children at Risk: Poverty and Disabilities,* T. Thompson and S. Hupp. (eds.). Newbury Park, Calif.: Sage.

Benard, B. 1992. Fostering resiliency in kids: Protective factors in the family, school, and community. *Illinois Prevention Forum* 12 (3): 1–16.

Berger, S., Shoul, R., and Warschauer, S. 1989. *Children of Divorce.* Washington, D.C.: National Education Association.

Bigner, J. 1985. *Parent-Child Relations.* New York: Macmillan.

Blazer, D. (ed.). 1989. *Faith Development in Early Childhood.* Kansas City, Mo.: Sheed and Ward.

Boss, P. 1988. *Family Stress Management.* Newbury Park, Calif.: Sage.

Boyer, E. 1991. *Ready to Learn: A Mandate for the Nation.* Princeton, N.J.: The Carnegie Foundation for the Advancement of Teaching.

Bradshaw, J. 1988. *The Family.* Pompano Beach, Fla: Health Communications.

Brickman, P., Kidder, L., Coates, D., Rabinowitz, V., Cohn, E., and Karuza, J. 1983. The dilemmas of helping: Making aid fair and effective. In *New Directions in Helping: Recipient Reactions to Aid,* vol. 1, J. Fisher, A. Nedler, and B. DePaulo (eds.). New York: Academic Press.

Brickman, P., Rabinowitz, V., Karuza, J., Coates, D., Cohn, E., and Kidder, L. 1982. Models of helping and coping. *American Psychologist* 37: 368–84.

Bronfenbrenner, U. 1986. Alienation and the four worlds of childhood. *Phi Delta Kappan* 67 (6): 430–36.

Bronfenbrenner, U. 1979. *The Ecology of Human Development.* Cambridge, Mass.: Harvard University Press.

Brooks, J. 1987. *The Process of Parenting.* Mountain View, Calif.: Mayfield.

Brophy, B. 1986. Children under stress. *U.S. News and World Report,* October 27, 58–64.

Brown, J. 1992. Maternal nutrition and the primary prevention of disabilities. In *Saving Children At Risk: Poverty and Disabilities,* T. Thompson and S. Hupp. (eds.). Newbury Park, Calif.: Sage.

Brown, L. 1987. Hunger in the United States. *Scientific American* 256 (2): 37–41.

Brubaker, T. (ed.). 1993. *Family Relations: Challenges for the Future.* Newbury Park, Calif.: Sage.

Burchard, J., and Burchard, S. 1987. *Prevention of Delinquent Behavior.* Newbury Park, Calif.: Sage.

Burgess, D., and Streissguth, A. 1992. Fetal alcohol syndrome and fetal alcohol effects: Principles for educators. *Phi Delta Kappan* 74 (1): 24–29.

Burland, J. 1984. Dysfunctional parenthood in a deprived population. In *Parenthood: A Psychodynamic Perspective,* R. Cohen, B. Cohler, and S. Weissman (eds.). New York: Guilford.

Caldwell, B. 1989. A faltering trust. In *Faith Development in Early Childhood,* D. Blazer. (ed.). Kansas City, Mo.: Sheed and Ward.

Calhoun, J. 1992. Youth as resources: A new paradigm in social policy for youth. In *Improving Children's Lives: Global Perspectives on Prevention,* G. Albee, L. Bond, and T. Monsey. (eds.). Newbury Park, Calif.: Sage.

Carkhuff, R., and Anthony, W. 1979. *The Skills of Helping.* Amherst, Mass.: Human Resource Development Press.

Cataldo, C. 1987. *Parent Education for Early Childhood.* New York: Teachers College Press.

Children's Defense Fund. 1987. *An Anatomy of a Social Problem: In Search of Comprehensive Solutions.* Washington, D.C.: Children's Defense Fund Adolescent Pregnancy Prevention Clearinghouse.

Children's Defense Fund. 1988. *A Children's Defense Fund Budget.* Washington, D.C.: Children's Defense Fund.

Children's Defense Fund. 1990. *S.O.S. America: A Children's Defense Budget.* Washington, D.C.: Children's Defense Fund.

Cochran, M. 1988. Parental empowerment in family matters: Lessons learned from a research program. In *Parent Education as Early Childhood Intervention,* D. Powell (ed.). Norwood, N.J.: Ablex.

Cochran, M., and Henderson, C. 1990. Network influences upon perception of the child: Solo parenting and social support. In *Extending Families: The Social Networks of Children and Their Families,* M. Cochran, M. Larner, D. Riley, L. Gunnarsson, and C. Henderson (eds.). New York: Cambridge University Press.

Cochran, M., and Henderson, C. 1985. *Family Matters: Evaluation of the Parental Empowerment Program.* Ithaca, N.Y.: Cornell University (Final Report to the National Institute of Education).

Cohen, S., and Syme, S. 1985. Issues in the study and application of social support. In *Social Support and Health,* S. Cohen and S. Syme (eds.). New York: Academic Press.

Cohen, S., and Taharally, C. 1992. Getting ready for young children with prenatal drug exposure. *Childhood Education* 69 (1): 5–9.

Comer, J., and Haynes, M. 1991. Parent involvement in schools: An ecological approach. *Elementary School Journal* 91, (3): 271–78.

Connell, D. 1987. The first 30 years were the fairest: Notes from the Kindergarten and Ungraded Primary (K-1-2). *Young Children* 42 (5): 30–39.

Cooperative Extension System, National Task Force on Youth At Risk. 1989. *Youth: The American Agenda.* Washington, D.C.: United States Department of Agriculture.

Cowan, C., and Cowan, P. 1992. *When Partners Become Parents: The Big Life Change for Couples.* New York: Basic Books.

Craig, S. 1992. The educational needs of children living with violence. *Phi Delta Kappan* 74 (1): 67–71.

Curran, D. 1985. *Stress and the Healthy Family.* Minneapolis, Minn.: Winston Press.

Darling, S. 1989. *Family Literacy Project.* Lousiville, Ky.: Kenan Family Literacy Project.

DeV. Peters, R., McMahon, R., and Quinsey, V. (eds.). 1992. *Aggression and Violence Throughout the Life Span.* Newbury Park, Calif.: Sage.

Dewey, J. 1916. *Democracy and Education.* New York: Macmillan.

Dimidjian, V. 1989. *Early Childhood At Risk.* Washington, D.C.: National Education Association.

Dorfman, C. (ed.). 1988. *Youth Indicators 1988: Trends in the Well-Being of American Youth.* Washington, D.C.: U.S. Department of Education.

Doyle, D. 1989. Endangered species: Children of promise. *Business Week.* Special Bonus Issue.

Dunst, C., and Leet, H. 1987. Measuring the adequacy of resources in households with young children. *Child: Child Care, Health, and Development,* 13: 111–25.

Dunst, C., Trivette, C., and Deal, A. 1988. *Enabling and Empowering Families: Principles and Guidelines for Practice.* Cambridge, Mass.: Brookline.

Edelman, M. 1987. *Families in Peril: An Agenda for Social Change.* Cambridge, Mass.: Harvard University Press.

Edelman, M. 1992. *The Measure of Our Success: A Letter to My Children and Yours.* Cambridge, Mass.: Harvard University Press.

Edmonds, R. 1986. Characteristics of effective schools. In *The School Achievement of Minority Children: New Perspectives,* R. Edmonds (ed.). Hillsdale, N.J.: Erlbaum Associates.

Edwards, P., and Young, L. 1992. Beyond parents: Family, community, and school involvement. *Phi Delta Kappan* 74 (1): 72–81.

Eisenberg, N. 1992. *The Caring Child.* Cambridge, Mass.: Harvard University Press.

Engstrom, L. 1988. The Minnesota experience with family-centered early childhood programs. *Community Education Journal,* (January): 312–14.

Enriquez, B. 1991. *Linkages and Transitions Between Early Childhood Education Programs and Kindergarten Grades.* El Paso, Tex.: Region XIX, Education Service Center.

Epstein, J., and Dauber, S. 1991. School programs and teacher practices of parent involvement in inner-city elementary and middle schools. *The Elementary School Journal* 91 (3): 289–306.

Erikson, E. 1959. *Identity and the Life Cycle.* New York: W.W. Norton.

Erikson, E. 1982. *The Life Cycle Completed: A Review.* New York: W.W. Norton.

Fisher, J., Nedler, A., and Whitcher-Alagna, S. 1983. Four theoretical approaches for conceptualizing reactions to aid. In *New Directions in Helping: Recipient Reactions to Aid,* vol. 1, J. Fisher, A. Nedler, and B. DePaulo (eds). New York: Academic Press.

Fontana, V. 1992. *Save the Family, Save the Child.* New York: Penguin (Mentor Edition).

Ford, D., and Lerner, R. 1992. *Developmental Systems Theory: An Integrative Approach.* Newbury Park, Calif.: Sage.

Fowler, J. 1989. Strength for the journey: Early childhood development in selfhood and faith. In *Faith Development in Early Childhood,* D. Blazer (ed.), Kansas City, Mo.: Sheed and Ward.

Fraiberg, L. (ed.). 1987. *Selected Writings of Selma Fraiberg.* Columbus, Ohio: Ohio State University Press.

Fraiberg, S. 1977. *Every Child's Birthright: In Defense of Mothering.* New York: Basic Books.

Frymier, J. 1991. *Learning to Fail: Case Studies of Students At Risk.* Bloomington, Ind.: Phi Delta Kappa.

Frymier, J. 1992. Children who hurt, children who fail. *Phi Delta Kappan* 74 (3): 257–59.

Furstenberg, E. 1985. Teenage parenthood and family support. In *Lives of Families,* K. Powers (ed.). Atlanta, Ga.: Humanics Limited.

Galinsky, E. 1990. Why are some teacher-parent relationships clouded with difficulties? *Young Children* 45 (5): 2–3, 38–39.

Galinsky, E. 1988. Parents and teachers/care givers: Sources of tension, sources of support. *Young Children* 43, (3): 4–12.

Galinsky, E. 1987. *The Six Stages of Parenthood.* Reading, Mass.: Addison-Wesley.

Gallagher, J., Beckman, P., and Cross, A. 1983. Families of handicapped children: Sources of stress and its amelioration. *Exceptional Children* 50: 10–19.

Garbarino, J. 1982. *Children and Families in the Social Environment.* New York: Aldine de Gruyter.

Gargiulo, R. 1985. *Working with Parents of Exceptional Children: A Guide for Professionals.* Boston, Mass.: Houghton Mifflin.

Garmezy, N. 1992. Resiliency and vulnerability to adverse developmental outcomes associated with poverty. In *Saving Children At Risk: Poverty and Disabilities,* T. Thompson and S. Hupp. (eds.). Newbury Park, Calif.: Sage.

Garmezy, N., and Rutter, M. 1983. *Stress, Coping, and Development in Children.* New York: McGraw-Hill.

Gelles, R., and Cornell, C. 1985. *Intimate Violence in Families.* Newbury Park, Calif.: Sage.

Gibbs, N. 1990. Shameful bequests to the next generation. *Time,* October 8, 41-48.

Gordon, I. 1977. *Building Effective Home-School Relationships.* Boston: Allyn and Bacon.

Gordon, I. 1975. *Research Report of Parent-Oriented Home-Based Early Childhood Education Programs.* Gainsville, Fla.: Institute for Human Development, University of Florida.

Gould, S. 1981. *The Mismeasure of Man.* New York: W.W. Norton.

Graves, S. 1990. *Social and Economic Issues Affecting Families.* Little Rock, Ark.: Southern Association on Children Under Six.

Graves, S., and Gargiulo, R. 1989. Parents and early childhood professionals as program partners: Meeting the needs of the preschool exceptional child. *Dimensions* 18 (1): 23–24.

Griffith, D. 1992. Prenatal exposure to cocaine and other drugs: Developmental and educational prognoses. *Phi Delta Kappan* 74 (1): 30–34.

Hale-Benson, J. 1986. *Black Children: Their Roots, Culture, and Learning,* revised edition. Baltimore, Md.: Johns Hopkins University Press.

Hall, A., and Wellman, B. 1985. Social networks and social support. In *Social Support and Health,* S. Cohen and S. Syme. (eds.). New York: Academic Press.

Halpern, R. 1987. Major social and demographic trends affecting young families: Implications for early childhood care and education. *Young Children* 42 (6): 34–40.

Hamburg, D. 1992. *Today's Children: Creating a Future for a Generation in Crisis.* New York: Random House (Times Books).

Hamner, T., and Turner, P. 1992. *Parenting in Contemporary Society,* (second edition). Englewood Cliffs, N.J.: Prentice-Hall.

Hampden-Turner, C. 1981. *Maps of the Mind.* New York: Macmillan.

Hetherington, M. 1979. Divorce: A child's perspective. *American Psychologist* 34: 851–58.

Hewlett, S. 1991. *When the Bough Breaks: The Cost of Neglecting Our Children.* New York: Basic Books.

Hilliard, A. 1976. *Alternatives to IQ Testing: An Approach to the Identification of Gifted Minority Children.* Sacramento, Calif.: California State Department of Education.

Honig, A. 1986. Stress and coping in children. *Young Children* 41, (4): 50–63.

Honig, A. 1989. The roots of faith: The crucial role of infant/toddler care givers. In *Faith Development in Early Childhood,* D. Blazer. (ed.). Kansas City, Mo.: Sheed and Ward.

Hunt, J. Mcv. 1961. *Intelligence and Experience.* New York: Ronald Press.

Hutchinson, J. 1991. What crack does to babies. *American Educator,* (Spring): 31-32.

Kagan, R., and Schlosberg, S. 1989. *Families in Perpetual Crisis.* New York: W.W. Norton.

Kaplan, L. (ed.). 1992. *Education and the Family.* Boston: Allyn and Bacon.

Karuza, J., Zevon, M., Rabinowitz, V., and Brickman, P. 1982. Attribution of responsibility by helpers and recipients. In *Basic Processes in Helping Relationships,* T. Wills. (ed.). New York: Academic Press.

Kerr, M., and Bowen, M. 1988. *Family Evaluation.* New York: W.W. Norton.

Kessler, M., Goldston, S., and Joffe, J. (eds.). 1992. *The Present and Future of Prevention.* Newbury Park, Calif.: Sage.

Kotre, J., and Hall, E. 1990. *Seasons of Life: Our Dramatic Journey from Birth to Death.* Boston: Little, Brown, and Company.

Kuhn, T. 1970. *The Structure of Scientific Revolutions.* Chicago: University of Chicago Press.

L'Abate, L. 1990. *Building Family Competence: Primary and Secondary Prevention Strategies*. Newbury Park, Calif.: Sage.

Langer, E. 1989. *Mindfulness*. Reading, Mass.: Addison-Wesley.

LaRossa, R. 1986. *Becoming a Parent*. Newbury, Calif.: Sage.

LeTendre, B. 1990. Implementing Accelerated Schools: Issues at the State Level. Presentation made at the American Educational Research Association Conference, Boston. (ERIC Document, ED 321 366.)

Levin, H. 1991. Building school capacity for effective teacher empowerment: Applications to elementary schools. (ERIC Document, ED 337 856.)

Lickona, T. 1992. *Educating for Character*. New York: Bantam Books.

Lightfoot, S. 1978. *Worlds Apart: Relationships Between Families and Schools*. New York: Basic Books.

Linehan, M. 1992. Children who are homeless: Educational strategies for school personnel. *Phi Delta Kappan* 74 (1): 61–66.

Magid, K., and McKelvey, C. 1987. *High Risk: Children Without a Conscience*. New York: Bantam Books.

Maslow, A. 1959. *New Knowledge in Human Values*. New York: Harper and Brothers.

Maslow, A. 1968. *Toward a Psychology of Being*. New York: D. Van Nostrand.

Milardo, R. 1988. *Families and Social Networks*. Newbury Park, Calif.: Sage.

Minuchin, S. 1984. *Family Kaleidoscope*. Cambridge, Mass.: Harvard University Press.

Newman, L., and Buka, S. 1991. Clipped wings. *American Educator*, Spring, 27–33.

Nichols, M. 1988. *The Power of the Family: Mastering the Hidden Dance of Family Relationships*. New York: Simon and Schuster.

Pence, A. 1988. *Ecological Research with Children and Families*. New York: Teachers College Press.

Piaget, J. 1954. *The Construction of Reality in the Child*. New York: Basic Books.

Pittman, F. 1987. *Turning Points: Treating Families in Transition and Crisis*. New York: W.W. Norton.

Popenoe, D. 1988. *Disturbing the Nest: Family Change and Decline in Modern Societies.* New York: Aldine de Gruyter.

Powell, D. (ed.). 1988. *Parent Education as Early Childhood Intervention.* Norwood, N.J.: Ablex.

Powell, D. 1989. *Families and Early Childhood Programs.* Washington, D.C.: National Association for the Education of Young Children.

Powers, K. 1985. *Lives of Families.* Atlanta, Ga.: Humanics.

*Primary Success: South Carolina's Plan to Redesign Primary Education.* 1992. Columbia, S.C.: South Carolina Department of Education.

Purkey, W., and Novak, J. 1984. *Inviting School Success: A Self-Concept Approach to Teaching and Learning.* Belmont, Calif.: Wadsworth.

Rabinowitz, V., Karuza, J., and Zevon, M. 1984. Fairness and effectiveness in premeditated helping. In *The Sense of Injustice,* R. Folger. (ed.). New York: Plenum.

Report of the National Task Force on School Readiness. 1992. *Caring Communities: Supporting Young Children and Families.* Alexandria, Va.: National Association of State Boards of Education.

Rich, D. 1987. *Schools and Families: Issues and Actions.* Washington, D.C.: National Education Association.

Rich, D. 1989. *Megaskills: How Families Can Help Children Succeed.* Boston: Houghton Mifflin.

Rohner, R. 1986. *The Warmth Dimension: Foundations of Parental Acceptance-Rejection Theory.* Newbury Park, Calif.: Sage.

Rossi, A., and Rossi, P. 1990. *Of Human Bonding.* New York: Aldine de Gruyter.

Rubin, S., and Quinn-Curran, N. 1983. Lost, then found: Parents journey through the community service maze. In *The Family with a Handicapped Child,* M. Seligman (ed.). New York: Grune and Stratton.

Rutter, M. 1987. Psychosocial resilience and protective mechanisms. *American Journal of Orthopsychiatry* 57: 316–31.

Sameroff, A., Barocas, R., and Seifer, R. 1985. Defining environmental risks: Multiple dimensions of psychological vulnerability. *American Journal of Community Psychology,* 13 (4): 433–47.

Sartain, H. 1989. *Nonachieving Students At Risk: School, Family, and Community Intervention.* Washington, D.C.: National Education

Association.

Schaefer, E. 1985. Parent and child correlates of parental modernity. In *Parental Belief Systems: The Psychological Consequences for Children,* I. Sigel (ed.). Hillsdale, N.J.: Erlbaum Associates.

Schaefer, E. 1991. Goals for parent and future-parent education: Research on parental beliefs and behavior. *The Elementary School Journal* 91 (3): 239–48.

Schorr, D., and Schorr, L. 1988. *Within Our Reach: Breaking the Cycle of Disadvantage.* New York: Doubleday.

Schultz, T., and Lombardi, J. 1992. Caring communities: Support young children and families. *Dimensions* 20 (1): 7–8.

Schwartzman, J. 1985. *Families and Other Systems.* New York: Guilford.

Seidel, J. 1992. Children with HIV-related developmental difficulties. *Phi Delta Kappan* 74 (1): 38–40.

Seligman, M. 1979. *Strategies for Helping Children of Exceptional Children.* New York: Free Press.

Shores, E. 1991. *Prenatal Cocaine Exposure: The South Looks for Answers.* Little Rock, Ark.: Southern Association on Children Under Six.

Sigel, I. (ed.). 1985. *Parental Belief Systems: The Psychological Consequences for Children.* Hillsdale, N.J.: Erlbaum Associates.

Skolnick, A. 1991. *Embattled Paradise: The American Family in an Age of Uncertainty.* New York: Basic Books.

Slavin, R., and Madden, N. 1989. What works for students at risk: A research synthesis. *Educational Leadership* (February): 4–12.

Spacapan, S., and Oskamp, S. (eds.). 1992. *Helping and Being Helped: Naturalistic Studies.* Newbury Park, Calif.: Sage.

Spivack, G., and Cianci, N. 1987. High-risk early behavior patterns and later delinquency. In *Prevention of Delinquent Behavior,* J. Burchard and S. Burchard (eds.). Newbury Park, Calif.: Sage.

Stark, W. 1992. Empowerment and social change: Health promotion within the Healthy Cities Project of WHO—Steps toward a participative prevention program. In *Improving Children's Lives: Global Perspectives on Prevention,* G. Albee, L. Bond, and T. Monsey (eds.). Newbury Park, Calif.: Sage.

Stern, D. 1977. *The First Relationship: Infant and Mother.* Cambridge, Mass.: Harvard University Press.

Stevens, L., and Price, M. 1992. Meeting the challenge of educating children at risk. *Phi Delta Kappan* 74 (1): 18–23.

Stinnett, N. 1979. *Building Family Strengths: Blueprints for Action.* Lincoln, Nebr.: University of Nebraska Press.

Stinnett, N. 1980. *Family Strengths: Positive Models for Family Life.* Lincoln, Nebr.: University of Nebraska Press.

Stinnett, N. 1981. *Family Strengths: Roots of Well-Being.* Lincoln, Nebr.: University of Nebraska Press.

Stinnett, N. 1982. *Family Strengths: Positive Support Systems.* Lincoln, Nebr.: University of Nebraska Press.

Stone, J. 1990. *Alcohol/Drug Abuse.* Washington, D.C.: National Education Association.

Swap, S. 1987. *Enhancing Parent Involvement in Schools.* New York: Teachers College Press.

Swick, K. 1984. *Inviting Parents into the Young Child's World.* Champaign, Ill.: Stipes.

Swick, K. 1987. *Perspectives on Understanding and Working with Families.* Champaign, Ill.: Stipes.

Swick, K. 1989. Strengthening families for the journey. In *Faith Development in Early Childhood,* D. Blazer (ed.). Kansas City, Mo.: Sheed and Ward.

Swick, K. 1991a. *First: A Rural Teacher-Parent Partnership for School Success.* Final report to the U.S. Office of Education (First Division), Columbia, South Carolina.

Swick, K. 1991b. *Teacher-Parent Partnerships to Enhance School Success in Early Childhood Education.* Washington, D.C.: National Education Association.

Swick, K. 1991c. *Discipline: Toward Positive Student Behavior.* Washington, D.C.: National Education Association.

Swick, K. 1992. *An Early Childhood School-Home Learning Design: Strategies and Resources.* Champaign, Ill: Stipes.

Swick, K., and Duff, E. 1982. *Involving Children in Parenting/Caring Experiences.* Dubuque, Iowa: Kendall Hunt.

Swick, K., and Graves S. 1986. Locus of control and interpersonal support as related to parenting. *Childhood Education* 62 (7): 26–31.

Swick, K., and McKnight, S. 1989. Characteristics of kindergarten teachers who promote parent involvement. *Early Childhood Research Quarterly* 4 (1): 19–30.

Thompson, T. 1992. For the sake of our children: Poverty and disabilities. In *Saving Children At Risk: Poverty and Disabilities,* T. Thompson and S. Hupp (eds.). Newbury Park, Calif.: Sage.

Thompson, T., and Hupp, S. (eds.). 1992. *Saving Children At Risk: Poverty and Disabilities.* Newbury Park, Calif.: Sage.

Thornburg, K., Hoffman, S., and Remeika, C. 1991. Youth at risk: Society at risk. *The Elementary School Journal* 91 (3): 199–208.

Tobin, J., Wu, D., and Davidson, D. 1989. *Preschool in Three Cultures.* New Haven, Conn.: Yale University Press.

Towers, R. 1989a. *Children of Alcoholics/Addicts.* Washington, D.C.: National Education Association.

Towers, R. 1989b. *Homeless Students.* Washington, D.C.: National Education Association.

U.S. Department of Education. 1988. *Youth Indicators 1988: Trends in the Well-Being of American Youth.* Washington, D.C.: Office of Educational Research and Improvement.

U.S. Department of Health and Human Services. 1992. *Healthy People 2000: National Health Promotion and Disease Prevention Objectives.* (Summary Report) Boston: Jones and Bartlett Publishers.

Viadero, D. 1989. Drug-exposed children pose special problems. *Education Week,* October 25, pp. 1, 10–11.

Weiss, F., and Jacobs, S. (eds.). 1988. *Evaluating Family Programs.* New York: Aldine de Gruyter.

Wells, K., and Biegel, D. 1991. *Family Preservation Services: Research and Evaluation.* Newbury Park, Calif.: Sage.

Werner, E. 1987. Vulnerability and resiliency in children at risk for delinquency: A longitudinal study from birth to young adulthood. In *Prevention of Delinquent Behavior,* J. Burchard and S. Burchard (eds.). Newbury Park, Calif.: Sage.

Weston, W. (ed.) 1989. *Education and the American Family.* New York: New York University Press.

White, B. 1988. *Educating the Infant and Toddler.* Lexington, Mass.: D.C. Heath.

Wilson, J., and Herrnstein, R. 1985. *Crime and Human Nature.* New York: Simon and Schuster.

Wolfe, D., Wekerle, C., and McGee, R. 1992. Developmental disparaties of abused children: Directions for prevention. In *Aggression and Violence Throughout the Life Span,* R.DeV. Peters, R. McMahon, and V. Quinsey (eds.). Newbury Park, Calif.: Sage.

Woolston, J. 1991. *Eating and Growth Disorders.* Newbury Park, Calif.: Sage.

Wright, J. 1989. *Address Unknown: The Homeless in America.* New York: Aldine de Gruyter.